**OPPOSING
VIEWPOINTS®
SERIES**

Male and Female Roles

Other Books of Related Interest:

Opposing Viewpoints Series

Girls and Sports

At Issue Series

Gay and Lesbian Families

Current Controversies Series

Homosexuality

"Congress shall make
no law . . . abridging
the freedom of speech,
or of the press."

First Amendment to the U.S. Constitution

The basic foundation of our democracy is the First Amendment guarantee of freedom of expression. The Opposing Viewpoints Series is dedicated to the concept of this basic freedom and the idea that it is more important to practice it than to enshrine it.

OPPOSING
VIEWPOINTS®
SERIES

Male and Female Roles

Karen Miller, Book Editor

GREENHAVEN PRESS
A part of Gale, Cengage Learning

GALE
CENGAGE Learning™

Detroit • New York • San Francisco • New Haven, Conn • Waterville, Maine • London

Christine Nasso, *Publisher*
Elizabeth Des Chenes, *Managing Editor*

For more information, contact:
Greenhaven Press
27500 Drake Rd.
Farmington Hills, MI 48331-3535
Or you can visit our Internet site at gale.cengage.com

For product information and technology assistance, contact us at

Gale Customer Support, 1-800-877-4253
For permission to use material from this text or product, submit all requests online at www.cengage.com/permissions

Further permissions questions can be emailed to permissionrequest@cengage.com

Articles in Greenhaven Press anthologies are often edited for length to meet page requirements. In addition, original titles of these works are changed to clearly present the main thesis and to explicitly indicate the author's opinion. Every effort is made to ensure that Greenhaven Press accurately reflects the original intent of the authors. Every effort has been made to trace the owners of copyrighted material.

Cover Image copyright Hans Neleman/The Image Bank/Getty Images.

LIBRARY OF CONGRESS CATALOGING-IN-PUBLICATION DATA

Male and female roles / Karen Miller, book editor.
   p. cm. -- (Opposing viewpoints)
   Includes bibliographical references and index.
   ISBN 978-0-7377-4528-3 (hardcover)
   ISBN 978-0-7377-4529-0 (pbk.)
   1. Sex role--Juvenile literature. I. Miller, Karen, 1973-
   HQ1075.M354 2009
   305.3--dc22

                                            2009019788

Contents

Chapter 3: How Do Gender Stereotypes Affect Perceptions of Men and Women?

Chapter 4: What Gender Roles Will Males and Females Play in the Future?

Why Consider Opposing Viewpoints?

> *"The only way in which a human being can make some approach to knowing the whole of a subject is by hearing what can be said about it by persons of every variety of opinion and studying all modes in which it can be looked at by every character of mind. No wise man ever acquired his wisdom in any mode but this."*
>
> John Stuart Mill

In our media-intensive culture it is not difficult to find differing opinions. Thousands of newspapers and magazines and dozens of radio and television talk shows resound with differing points of view. The difficulty lies in deciding which opinion to agree with and which "experts" seem the most credible. The more inundated we become with differing opinions and claims, the more essential it is to hone critical reading and thinking skills to evaluate these ideas. Opposing Viewpoints books address this problem directly by presenting stimulating debates that can be used to enhance and teach these skills. The varied opinions contained in each book examine many different aspects of a single issue. While examining these conveniently edited opposing views, readers can develop critical thinking skills such as the ability to compare and contrast authors' credibility, facts, argumentation styles, use of persuasive techniques, and other stylistic tools. In short, the Opposing Viewpoints Series is an ideal way to attain the higher-level thinking and reading skills so essential in a culture of diverse and contradictory opinions.

In addition to providing a tool for critical thinking, Opposing Viewpoints books challenge readers to question their own strongly held opinions and assumptions. Most people form their opinions on the basis of upbringing, peer pressure, and personal, cultural, or professional bias. By reading carefully balanced opposing views, readers must directly confront new ideas as. well as the opinions of those with whom they disagree. This is not to simplistically argue that everyone who reads opposing views will—or should—change his or her opinion. Instead, the series enhances readers' understanding of their own views by encouraging confrontation with opposing ideas. Careful examination of others' views can lead to the readers' understanding of the logical inconsistencies in their own opinions, perspective on why they hold an opinion, and the consideration of the possibility that their opinion requires further evaluation.

Evaluating Other Opinions

To ensure that this type of examination occurs, Opposing Viewpoints books present all types of opinions. Prominent spokespeople on different sides of each issue as well as well-known professionals from many disciplines challenge the reader. An additional goal of the series is to provide a forum for other, less known, or even unpopular viewpoints. The opinion of an ordinary person who has had to make the decision to cut off life support from a terminally ill relative, for example, may be just as valuable and provide just as much insight as a medical ethicist's professional opinion. The editors have two additional purposes in including these less known views. One, the editors encourage readers to respect others' opinions—even when not enhanced by professional credibility. It is only by reading or listening to and objectively evaluating others' ideas that one can determine whether they are worthy of consideration. Two, the inclusion of such viewpoints encourages the important critical thinking skill of objectively evaluating an author's credentials and bias. This evaluation will illuminate an author's reasons for taking a particular stance on an issue and will aid in readers' evaluation of the author's ideas.

It is our hope that these books will give readers a deeper understanding of the issues debated and an appreciation of the complexity of even seemingly simple issues when good and honest people disagree. This awareness is particularly important in a democratic society such as ours in which people enter into public debate to determine the common good. Those with whom one disagrees should not be regarded as enemies but rather as people whose views deserve careful examination and may shed light on one's own.

Thomas Jefferson once said that "difference of opinion leads to inquiry, and inquiry to truth." Jefferson, a broadly educated man, argued that "if a nation expects to be ignorant and free . . . it expects what never was and never will be." As individuals and as a nation, it is imperative that we consider the opinions of others and examine them with skill and discernment. The Opposing Viewpoints Series is intended to help readers achieve this goal.

David L. Bender and Bruno Leone,
Founders

Introduction

> *"If a few women of character and recognized position would only follow me, Wall Street would very soon be opened up as a field for the activities of women, and I think they would succeed in it. Their perceptions are quicker than those of men, and, popular belief to the contrary notwithstanding, they are less easily influenced. The chief difficulty with a woman is that she has a tendency to become excited when things are going her way and to carry her operations too far."*
>
> *Anonymous female*
> *stock broker interviewed in*
> *the New York Times, March 26, 1893*

It would hardly be an exaggeration to say that the health of the modern economy lies in the hands of the stockbrokers and analysts who populate Wall Street in New York City and the financial districts of major cities around the world. They are the "Masters of the Universe"—men in expensive suits who shout into telephones, fight for position on the trading floor, and work long hours every day of the week. It is an incomplete image, of course. Women also work as stockbrokers and traders and do the same work and make the same decisions as their male counterparts.

Women stockbrokers are often omitted from the picture because they are so few in number. Clifton Green, Narasimhan Jegadeesh, and Yue Tang, authors of the article "Gender and Job Performance: Evidence from Wall Street," calculated that in 2005, only 13 percent of all financial analysts were female. Although gender imbalances exist in many industries (only a few generations of women have started careers since the feminist movement of the 1960s and 1970s), women are grossly underrepresented in finance. Part of the imbalance is caused by women who leave to start families and cannot easily return to the long hours required by many firms. Another part of the disparity can be attributed to the fact that women simply do not choose this career as often as men do. Even in the twenty-first century, Wall Street is a man's world, and not enough research has been conducted to discern whether artificial barriers are keeping women from thriving there or whether the industry merely appeals more to males.

Preliminary studies, however, have yielded provocative results. Researchers John Coates and Joe Herbert measured the testosterone levels of seventeen male stockbrokers and discovered that high levels of testosterone correlated to highly profitable days of trading. The more testosterone these men had in their system at 11:00 A.M. (when samples were taken), the better they performed. Raised testosterone levels made the men more competitive, quicker to act, and more willing to take big risks that paid big dividends. These findings raise the question of whether testosterone-deficient people (such as women) are at an actual physical disadvantage to men in financial careers. Testosterone levels have no relationship to the amount of information and experience a person has about financial markets and trends, but they could influence how quickly a trader reacts to new information. The industry is volatile; decisions are made rapidly and too much hesitation can cost an investor millions of dollars, leading some to wonder whether women even belong in this field at all.

New York Times columnist Nicholas Kristof argues they do—in fact Wall Street needs more women, he believes. His opinion piece, "Mistresses of the Universe," considers how Coates and Herbert's findings underscore the global economic recession: highly charged men in very homogenous gender groups egg each other on to very risky, very shortsighted financial behaviors—the kind of behaviors that make retirement funds disappear and real estate prices tumble overnight. Bereft of testosterone levels as high as those of their male counterparts, female stockbrokers make fewer hormonally driven decisions. Kristof takes note of another study's findings that the outrageous risks that make outrageous fortunes can just as easily result in spectacular failures.

As Kristof further explains, a better balance of genders makes a group smarter. The more homogenous a group is, the worse it solves problems—especially economic ones. On Wall Street, it's not just that men are influenced by testosterone to behave in adventurous, bold ways; single-gender groups do not make decisions as thoughtfully or as skillfully as mixed-gender groups because they operate within a single frame of reference. (According to this logic, all-female investment firms would perform as poorly as all-male ones.) The findings in these studies have led some to conclude that recruiting and retaining female stockbrokers in greater numbers at the male-dominated firms operating today may lessen the occurrence of extreme risk-taking, and a better gender balance could improve a firm's capability to address the needs of its clients, the variances of the market, and the making of responsible investments.

In addition, a deliberate effort to install women in investment firms would expand women's roles in the global economy, from consumers to decision makers. Until very recently, women held no positions of financial oversight, yet the world has seen eras of profound prosperity as well as deep depression; maybe gender balance is irrelevant. On the other hand, advancements in communication technologies and the increasing democratization of the world's countries have drastically increased the rate of trade and the numbers of transactions. The scale of the economy is magnified beyond anything in history, and the variables that affect market trends are too numerous to comprehend without computers.

The economy is more difficult to understand today. It needs better financial experts making better decisions. Investment firms, and the society that patronizes them, will have to decide whether the best way to find success will be to deliberately hire women to create a gender balance or to consider each candidate for experience and aptitude, no matter the gender of the talent.

Opposing Viewpoints: Male and Female Roles explores how the biological and social roles played by males and females influence men, women, and society, and describes in the following four chapters some of the cultural and political aspects of these distinct gender roles: Are Male and Female Roles Biologically Derived? What Are Some Cultural Effects of Male and Female Roles? How Do Gender Stereotypes Affect Perceptions of Men and Women? and What Gender Roles Will Males and Females Play in the Future? This book focuses on what extent biological differences determine gender behaviors and how social opportunity, intellectual ability, and personal inclination liberates them.

OPPOSING VIEWPOINTS® SERIES

CHAPTER 1

Are Male and Female Roles Biologically Derived?

Chapter Preface

In 1975, biologist Edward O. Wilson published his book *Sociobiology: The New Synthesis* and popularized a new scientific field of research. Trained as an entomologist who specialized in ants, Wilson wrote about how biology influences social behavior across species, including humans. Although the term "sociobiology" had been coined in the 1940s, Wilson used it to describe a synthesis of many different sciences, from ecology to genetics, that investigated why animals do what they do.

Sociobiology seeks to explain all aspects of animal activities and preferences, suggesting biological and evolutionary origins for behaviors ranging from fear of snakes (early mammals evolved around dangerous reptiles) to why landscapes with wide-open spaces, the occasional tree, and water features are so popular (humans evolved on the savannahs of Africa). Evolutionary psychology, the branch of sociobiology that addresses the evolutionary origins of human mental and psychological processes, seeks biological explanations for documented differences between male and female behaviors.

For example, research suggests men are better than women at spatial awareness tasks, such as reading maps or identifying objects that have been rotated. One evolutionary psychology explanation for this disparity is that because women bore and raised children, they were not available to hunt; men took on this responsibility, and skilled fathers passed down to their descendents the ability to track animals and throw spears. Similarly, studies show women to be better at verbal and social interpretation tasks; nonhunting women interacted with each other and cooperated on tasks such as preparing group meals and working skins and leather for shelter and warmth. The better communicators secured more help and resources for their children. The joke about men never being able to find something in the refrigerator can be traced back to women gathering plants for food and learning how to spot tiny leaves and seeds among a vast backdrop of greenery, while men sought larger moving targets. Evolutionary psychology says that over hundreds of thousands of years, proclivities for such activities—separated by sex because of the biological realities of pregnancy and nursing—became hardwired into human brains.

The claims of sociobiology and evolutionary psychology are not without controversy, however. First and foremost, although these fields draw on scientific knowledge and practices, they cannot seek data via replicable experiments; how can you re-create ancient history? Philosophers and academics especially object to the biologically determined explanations for behavior put forth by sociobiologists. Critics argue that the field is just a fancy way of championing nature in the nature-versus-nurture debate, which has been used throughout history and across cultures to support the assertion that biological differences make some people—especially women and members of minority groups—unfit to perform certain work. Conversely, the "nurture" faction argues that cultural attitudes really determine what males and females are taught to do and how to behave.

Researchers in the field of sociobiology claim they are just searching for answers about why people do what they do, not about what people ought to do. If females evolved a good eye for telling colors apart because they spent so much time searching for edible plants instead of hunting, then that's what happened. It doesn't mean a man can't become a good interior decorator and it doesn't mean that a woman can't learn to throw a football. Biological propensities notwithstanding, men and women still have to learn the tasks their prehistoric ancestors had to learn. On the other hand, there are fewer male than female interior decorators and fewer football leagues for females than males. Is this socially significant? Does recognizing differences in the innate abilities and interests of men and women devalue their chosen pursuits?

The following chapter addresses the gender divide in the activities and responsibilities of modern life and explores whether men and women are biologically suited for certain roles—or whether it even matters.

| "There [is] a disconnect between gender role attitudes and gender role performance [because of] differences in innate male and female preferences."

Biology Contributes to Differences Between Male and Female Behaviors

Steven E. Rhoads

Steven E. Rhoads has taught public policy at the University of Virginia for more than thirty years. His essays have appeared in the New York Times, Public Interest, *and other publications. The following viewpoint is from his book* Taking Sex Differences Seriously, *which argues that men and women fall into different social and familial roles for biological reasons and because of human nature. In the viewpoint, Rhoads reveals the disparity between how much child care mothers and fathers actually perform despite the facts that men and women say it should be shared equally and mothers are as intensely focused on their professional careers as fathers are.*

As you read, consider the following questions:

1. According to the author, how did male and female academics tend to answer questions about which parent should be responsible for child care?

2. How did male and female academics tend to actually divide the responsibilities of child care, as cited by Rhoads?

3. According to the author, how is paid leave for child care benefiting male academics and penalizing female ones?

If gender identities have changed dramatically, we would see it most clearly among the junior ranks of university faculties. A number of studies indicate that university faculty have less stereotypical understandings of gender roles than do most Americans. For example, though they may not always demonstrate common sense, most academics have been among the brightest students in their high schools, and research shows that intellectually gifted high school students, whether measured by IQ or academic achievement, have less stereotypical personalities, interests and behaviors than others of their sex.

There is other evidence suggesting that academics should be more androgynous than the norm, possessing a mix of masculine and feminine traits. One study finds that both women with jobs and women with college degrees score lower on femininity (gender-related personality traits) than do other women. Moreover, their husbands score somewhat lower on masculinity scales. Another study of women finds that younger age and advanced degrees are both associated with egalitarian gender role attitudes. And still another study finds that "the *expression* of high intellectual ability is linked to the rejection of 'traditional' sex-role ideology."

Attitudes aside, advanced degrees and professional status seem to be associated with a more equal parental distribution of baby care and of domestic work in general. Professors, of course, have advanced degrees and professional status. Moreover, compared with most Americans, university faculty are much more likely to have spouses with advanced degrees and professional status. Thus we would expect men in academic families to do more child care than other men.

With this in mind, I initiated a nationwide study of how male and female faculty members use parental leave. Our research team conducted lengthy phone interviews with 184 assistant professors (109 men and 75 women) trying to obtain tenure—the holy grail of academic job security—while simultaneously raising a child under age two. We wanted to learn about differences in the frequency with which male and female faculty took advantage of paid leave opportunities after the births of their babies, how much child care each did compared with the spouse, and how they felt about the baby care experience and about gender roles more generally.

Expectations of Equality

More male child care might seem especially likely among those men married to the female professors in our study. These women are serious careerists. The schools that offer paid postbirth leave are generally the rich ones, those ranked among the top colleges and universities in the country. Female assistant professors who have gained appointments at such institutions are typically bright, hard-working and ambitious. If they do not have enough time to do research during their probationary period, they will not achieve tenure. Thus, as two scholars put it, "[If there is] any occupational group in which the ideology of gender equality would be expected to develop sooner than the general population, it would be female college faculty." Husbands of female faculty are also aware of their wives' career requirements and should be more likely than most men to help with baby and toddler care.

In our study, we asked the professors how strongly they agreed or disagreed with the following statement: "Families usually do best if the husband and wife share equally in child care, household work, and paid work." Here is what we found. Over 75 percent of female faculty agreed with this statement, and less than 10 percent disagreed. Male faculty were less supportive, 55 percent agreeing with the statement and 33 percent disagreeing. (Some respondents said they neither agreed nor disagreed.) Although there is a significant difference in responses, it is striking that majorities of both sexes agreed with a statement strongly in support of equal gender roles in child care.

Reality Belies Expectations

The actual performance of child care tasks, however, did not reflect the professors' intellectual commitments. To start with, the men did not often take the offered leave that might have made equal care of their newborns possible. Whereas 67 percent of eligible female faculty took the paid leave available to them, only 12 percent of male faculty took postbirth leave.

Leave-taking aside, we measured child care effort by specifying twenty-five child care tasks and asking whether they were always or usually done by the respondent, always or usually done by the spouse, or done equally. The tasks encompassed items that assess the division of parental responsibility for basic care (e.g., care when sick, changing diapers); logistics (e.g., taking the child to paid day care or buying food or toys); consulting and planning (e.g., seeking and implementing advice about child care or managing the division of labor for child care); recreation (e.g., playing with the child, taking child for walk in stroller); and emotional involvement (e.g., comforting the child when he/she is upset).

Female academics, on average, did all twenty-five of the tasks far more often than male academics. Gender differences in the amount of child care performed remained extremely large when we compared separately the male and female leave takers on the one hand, and those who did not take leave on the other. While those males who took leave had ample opportunity to participate in child care and did so more than males who took no leave, they still did significantly less baby and toddler care on average than females in either group, those who took leave and those who did not.

If we look only at those faculty who say they believe that child care should be shared equally, we again find that women with this egalitarian attitude do more than half the care, whereas men with these beliefs do less that half. The sex differences in responses were again quite large. More specifically, by their own reports, none of the six men who took leave, had an egalitarian gender ideology and were married to women with full-time jobs did as much as half the baby and toddler care. In fact, taken as a whole, less than 3 percent of our male respondents said they did more child care than their spouses, whereas 96 percent of female faculty said they did more.

Seeking Explanations in Biological Differences

Why is there such a disconnect between gender role attitudes and gender role performance? I think that differences in innate male and female preferences are at least partly responsible. We asked our faculty how much they liked doing the twenty-five baby/toddler care tasks (*liked a lot; liked somewhat; neither liked nor disliked; disliked somewhat; disliked a lot*). The sex differences here were not as large as the differences in the amount of child care performed; nonetheless, the existence of sex differences was unmistakable. Female faculty liked doing 24 of the 25 tasks more than male faculty, and for 16 of the 25 tasks, this difference was large.

The one task that the men liked to do more than the women was managing the division of labor of parenting tasks. Except for getting up at night to care for the child, this was the task that women liked least, perhaps because taking on this task led to tension or arguments with their husbands.

Males and Females Behave Differently from Birth

Many researchers have described disparities in how "people-centered" male and female infants are. For example, [University of Cambridge professor Simon] Baron-Cohen and his student Svetlana Lutchmaya found that one-year-old girls spend more time looking at their mothers than boys of the same age do. And when these babies are presented with a choice of films to watch, the girls look longer at a film of a face, whereas boys lean toward a film featuring cars.

Of course, these preferences might be attributable to differences in the way adults handle or play with boys and girls. To eliminate this possibility, Baron-Cohen and his students went a step further. They took their video camera to a maternity ward to examine the preferences of babies that were only one day old. The infants saw either the friendly face of a live female student or a mobile that matched the color, size and shape of the student's face and included a scrambled mix of her facial features. To avoid any bias, the experimenters were unaware of each baby's sex during testing. When they watched the tapes, they found that the girls spent more time looking at the student, whereas the boys spent more time looking at the mechanical object. This difference in social interest was evident on day one of life—implying again that we come out of the womb with some cognitive sex differences built in.

Larry Cahill,
Scientific American, *April 25, 2005.*

The survey revealed other evidence that women like baby care very much. Of the 72 women who breastfed their child,

71 indicated that they enjoyed it. For the set of twenty-five questions measuring enjoyment of all the child care tasks, only 2 percent of the total female responses indicated a strong dislike for a task. Only 14 percent of the time did women indicate a moderate dislike for a task. In other words, to the extent that female responses varied on the appeal of child care, the variation was usually between indifference and great enjoyment. There was relatively little indication of actual dislike. Women often indicated liking what to most men seem disagreeable tasks, such as changing the child's diapers. Over half of the women enjoyed this task, while two times as many men disliked it as liked it.

One reason that women may like baby and toddler care more than men do is that the children respond more favorably to a mother's care. We asked our respondents if the child seemed to have a preference about whom he played with and who comforted him. There were essentially no differences with respect to playing, but the children had an overwhelming preference for being comforted by their mothers. All in all, when the babies had a preference, the babies and toddlers preferred their mothers to their fathers by fourteen to one. Even among men who took leave, the children were twice as likely, by their fathers' reports, to want to be comforted by their mothers.

Women Balance Work and Family

Academic women seem to enjoy baby and toddler care. Our survey shows that they also love their jobs and they care almost as much about getting tenure as the male faculty do. Yet these women are dramatically more likely to have thought about dropping off the tenure track or getting out of the academic world entirely because of the pressures of balancing work and family. Fully half of all female professors in the survey responded that they had considered leaving the tenure track, while only 27 percent of the male professors had thought of doing so. Additionally, academic women are nearly twice as likely as the men to report feeling overwhelmed by their responsibilities as a parent and are much more likely to report that the division of child care labor in the family is unfair to them.

Paid postbirth leave originally appeared in academia as a way to help level the playing field for young women trying to get tenure while raising children. But the women's movement has insisted on policy that resists stereotypes and encourages men to take on a larger share of parenting. As a result, most of the professors in our survey were at institutions that allowed both fathers and mothers to take paid postbirth leave.

Despite what they said about the importance of sharing child-rearing, these male professors, who by all rights should be more egalitarian than most men, were not often taking leave, nor were they doing intensive baby care in the way that the female professors were. Indeed, there is reason to think that our formal results overstate how much of it the male faculty actually do. When we debriefed our phone interviewers, they said that the men often seemed embarrassed when they kept answering that their wives always or usually did the specific child care tasks we enumerated. Half way through the list, one guy joked, "I don't sound too good here, do I?" Another admitted, "If I were completely honest, I would look like a bad parent." Some men even interrupted their string of "she does it more" answers with editorials to the effect that their wives were more emotionally suited to baby care. The interviewers on the survey came to believe that many of the men were also defensive on the questions about enjoying baby care and were saying they liked it more than they really did because they were embarrassed to tell the truth.

Men Benefit from Child Care Leave

We heard stories of male academics who took paid postbirth leave in order to advance their publishing agendas. One top university had to change its rules in an effort to minimize this behavior. Some assistant professors were taking leave even though their wives didn't have jobs. Another had taken leave while his child was in full-time day care. At my own university, a young female colleague has told me of similar instances of male abuse of the policy at the school where she received her Ph.D. She also recalls a revealing conversation with a male colleague upon her return from postbirth leave. He asked how the leave had gone, and she replied, "I used the time well." Then the man said, "So you got a lot of work done"—a statement that did not reflect what she meant at all.

One woman gave this answer to an open-ended request for further thoughts about tenure-track professors facing parenthood: "If women and men are both granted parental leaves and women recover/nurse/do primary care and men do some care and finish articles, there's a problem, though a problem with no clear solution."

Solutions would become clearer if we took sex differences seriously. Our study of parental leave in academia shows that despite egalitarian gender ideologies, almost none of our male faculty, including male leave takers, do half the baby care. Even the three men (out of 109) who say they *do* perform half the work are not simultaneously recovering from pregnancy and delivery as their female counterparts are. Moreover, none of them is breastfeeding, a task more time-consuming and physically draining than any of the other tasks in the survey.

Refusal to take sex differences seriously, rather than helping women, leads to a policy that could injure those seeking tenure by giving their male counterparts an unfair advantage. If men should begin to take leave in much larger numbers, far from leveling the playing field, gender-neutral postbirth leaves will tilt the field further in favor of men.

"*Gay men and lesbians . . . perform varying degrees of masculinity and femininity in relation to their partner in the home, particularly in the way they engage with domestic labour.*"

Biology Does Not Contribute to Differences Between Male and Female Behaviors

Susan Kentlyn

Susan Kentlyn is a postgraduate researcher in the school of social science at Queensland University in Australia and the 2006 recipient of the John Western Sociology Prize. In the following viewpoint, Kentlyn explores how gay and lesbian domestic couples who have lived together for more than two years distribute household chores and maintenance. She asks if these couples group tasks along heteronormative lines—that is, does one person do the cooking and cleaning ("female" tasks) and the other person the yard work and fixing things ("male" tasks)—and what homosexual partnerships reveal about the biological relationship of gender to domestic interests.

Susan Kentlyn, "'Who's the Man and Who's the Woman?' Same-Sex Couples in Queensland 'Doing' Gender and Domestic Labor," *Queensland Review*, vol. 14, 2007, pp. 111–124. Copyright © 2007 University of Queensland Press. Reproduced by permission.

As you read, consider the following questions:

1. With what gender do gay and lesbian couples classify domestic work, according to Kentlyn?

2. Why does the author compare establishing a gender identity to adjusting the treble and the bass on the stereo?

3. How do lesbian and gay couples distribute their household tasks, according to the author?

In looking at how lesbian and gay people engage with household chores, I was interested to discover whether they reproduce heteronormative gender roles with their associated patterns of domestic labour—in other words, does one take a conventional masculine role with little *responsibility* for the work of the household, and does the other take a conventional feminine role with almost total responsibility for family work? If this is not the case, can other styles of sharing and factors affecting the allocation of tasks be identified?

Of special interest to me was the role, if any, of gender. Can [Sarah Fenstermaker] Berk's contention [in her 1985 book, *The Gender Factory*] that doing domestic labour is a way of 'doing' femininity be applied to couples where both are ostensibly of the same gender? This would seem to provide an opportunity to examine gender outside the 'heterosexual matrix' with ramifications for gender theory in general, and the individual practice of gender in particular. Therefore this examination will focus on several key questions, outlined below.

Same-Sex Couples and Traditional Gender Roles

David: . . . a lot of people who know I'm gay, I've been surprised how many say, well, *which one of you's the man and which one of you's the woman?* [emphasis added]

David's friends are not alone in this expectation—many of the couples have been confronted by the same question. Of the 12 couples interviewed, none displayed a gender presentation and division of domestic labour that reflected normative heterosexual gender roles. Most of the partners enacted very similar gender styles in terms of outward presentation, with almost all hovering around a fairly androgynous style. Amongst the lesbians there was one couple who were butch/ femme in appearance, Robyn and Chris, but Chris—the butch-looking one—owned all the delicate glass ornaments, and she also did the majority of the domestic labour. Most of the couples showed an awareness that their status as gay and lesbian people made them 'gender outlaws'—some even took pride in that fact.

Interviewer: Home maintenance. If something breaks, who fixes it? Is there a power tool queen in the family?

Cameron: I don't think we have one. There's a food processor [laughs]. We're so gay! [laughs]

This makes the negotiation of domestic labour unavoidable.

Ian: . . . when there are two men involved in any case, then I can't see how anybody has the right to feel that they're more masculine than the other person, when we're both two males, we're both sexually the same, we both have penises and so forth, and whatever role we play we might outshine the other in doing other things which are thought of as being the man's role or the woman's role.

Int: . . . it's not like one takes the woman's role, one takes the man's role, it's more like interchangeable?

Ian: Definitely not. Interchangeable. Yes.

Int: . . . a lot of men find it difficult to do housework because it seems to threaten their sense of their masculinity. That's never been an issue for either of you?

Ian's partner, Andrew, summarised the bottom line succinctly:

Andrew: No. Too bad if we did. If we don't do it, who's going to?

In their accounts of domestic labour, none of the respondents attributed the way the tasks were allocated or performed to heteronormative gender roles—what [researchers J.] Goodnow and [J.] Bowes describe as 'women do all the "inside" house jobs, while men do all the "outside" work and only that.' In fact, most expressed some degree of repugnance for what they perceived as the rigidity of gender roles in heterosexual relationships in general, and marriage in particular. . . .

Gender Roles Are Continual Performances

In this study, because both partners are of the same gender, I initially assumed that gender would not be a factor in domestic labour. However, the more interviews I conducted, the more it became apparent to me that same-sex partners do not necessarily perform the same gender as each other. Indeed, in the private space of the queer home and in the negotiation and performance of domestic labour, gender is still produced, even if it does not take the form of conventional understandings of masculinity and femininity.

Clearly most of the respondents, both female and male, viewed domestic labour as closely aligned with femininity, low in status, and particularly susceptible to power relations of dominance and subordination.

Luke: . . . with [gay] male relationships, one person is often assumed to be the one to do that role . . . to be the woman, and I find that whole patriarchal thing just a bit annoying because it says that women cook and clean and do this and that, so ironically I probably refuse to participate by not doing a lot of cooking and cleaning and stuff because I think, that's just crap. . . .

Int: An expectation on the part of your partner, or of other people?

Allocating Chores in Same-Sex Households

Name of Factor	Description
Preference	Jobs people enjoy doing, or find least objectionable.
Aversion	Jobs people dislike so much they either refuse to do them, or are more likely to neglect them.
Time at home	Those who spend more time at home are seen as able to do more household labour—within limits.
Time at home during the day	Shift workers who spend more time at home during the day may find themselves doing more domestic labour.
Health	Health problems may limit the type of activities a partner can do, or the tempo with which they are done.
Skills	Superior levels of skill can lead to one partner taking ownership of a particular task.
Standards	The partner with higher standards may take responsibility for a task to ensure their standards are met.
Zone	One zone of the house becomes the particular responsibility of one partner.

TAKEN FROM: Susan Kentlyn, "'Who's the Man and Who's the Woman?' Same Sex Couples in Queensland 'Doing' Gender and Domestic Labour," *Queensland Review*, vol. 14, no. 2 (2007), pp. 111–124. Copyright © 2007 by University of Queensland Press. Reprinted with permission.

Luke: Um, on the part of the partner . . . that one person generally does the girlie stuff. And that would be how they phrase it . . . the woman's work . . . it's just the oppressive part of it . . . that women are meant to do it. Not that women do it, but that they're *meant* to do it . . . it's just that whole, I guess, expectation that women . . . definitely do more . . . that women do certain roles, and that men do them only if they're helping out, or being . . . in some way, feminised, which is always seen as a negative. . . .

The gay men showed widely different attitudes to embracing what Luke called a 'feminised' identity through performing 'women's work', and this demonstrated the kind of gender they enacted. I would argue that I was seeing many different kinds of gay masculinity. From their accounts, I further discerned that the kind of masculinity produced in the home could be quite different from that evinced in other social spaces, such as the workplace, and in different intimate relationships; individuals often reported that their practice of domestic labour was different in other cohabiting same-sex partnerships.

I conceptualise the process by means of an analogy to the modulation of sound, such that doing gender is like adjusting the balance between bass (conventionally masculine behaviours, attitudes and attributes) and treble (conventionally feminine behaviours, attitudes and attributes). This brings with it an understanding that gender does not fall into discrete categories, such as 'hegemonic masculinity' or 'emphasised femininity,' butch or femme. Rather, each person adjusts the degree of masculinity or femininity they do in particular contexts and in relation to other people. A person of any gender can turn up their 'treble'—femininity—not only by means of wearing female clothing or accentuating conventional aspects of female embodiment, such as high voice and gestures, but also by engaging in 'female' jobs, such as nursing or child care, and 'female' behaviours—in this case, doing indoor domestic labour. Similarly, a person of any gender can turn up their 'bass'—masculinity—by wearing male clothing or accentuating typically male aspects of male embodiment, such as deep voice, hairiness, upper body strength, but also by engaging in 'male jobs' such as truck driving or engineering, and 'male' behaviours, such as contact sports, working on cars or doing 'outdoor' forms of domestic labour. This process has been masked in heterosexual households because the male-bodied partner is made primarily responsible for the performance of masculinity and the female-bodied partner for femininity. In same-sex households, the continuously shifting and negotiated nature of this performance is made apparent. Gay men and lesbians may be seen to perform varying degrees of masculinity and femininity in relation to their partner in the home, particularly in the way they engage with domestic labour; these same people may adjust the balance of masculine and feminine behaviours in different contexts, such as work or sport, and in relation to other people, such as friends, coworkers or other family members. . . .

Public Appearance Affects Private Behavior

Max and his partner Dennis are what's known as 'bears'—tall, barrel-chested, hirsute, with deep, resonant voices—blokey but gentle. Max says that people in his workplace do not guess that he is gay because he does not fit the usual gay stereotype. At home, however, it is a different matter—the guys are into interior decoration, pastry cooking, scrapbooking, visual arts, preserves; their place in a northern beachside suburb looks like a spread from *Home Beautiful*. Besides being conventionally masculine in appearance, one of the other gay men, Grant, plays Rugby and goes to the gym; he seems to have no problem with taking on the menial jobs of cleaning, leaving the kitchen to his partner, Alan. Thus the more conventionally masculine the gay men appear to be, the more latitude it appears to give them to 'turn up' the feminine dimensions of their personality without forfeiting a masculine identity.

Conversely, Luke and Scott own an apartment in the trendy inner-city suburb known as Brisbane's 'gay ghetto'. In appearance they are short, slightly built and metrosexual, with gestures and voices that evoke the stereotype of the 'effeminate' gay. However, [gender studies author Robert] Connell's 'very straight gay' is also much in evidence—they spend hours each day on sport and exercise: swimming, martial arts, cycling and gym workouts. Scott tried to avoid any discussion of the minutiae of domestic labour, breezily maintaining that the cleaning lady did everything. Luke has already been quoted about his resistance to doing 'feminine' jobs and thus taking on a feminised identity. Their 'treble' is already set so high, in terms of their gender presentation, that they seem to need to turn up their 'bass' by means of sport and exercise, and not turn up their 'treble' any further by being seen to engage in feminine tasks, so as not to forfeit their masculine identity. Similarly, Ian, who is much more effeminate in his gender presentation than his partner Andrew, has never done any cleaning chores. Andrew says: 'Ian wouldn't know what end of the vacuum cleaner is what!'

Women Performing and Rejecting Traditional Roles

The modulation of gender performance in lesbian couples appears much more complex, driven by many competing factors and conflicted desires. The women seemed to be torn by the need to acknowledge the value of 'women's work' whilst also seeing it as symbolic of women's oppression and position of subordination within gendered relations of power. Some saw it as embodying an ethos of care for those they loved, even while they may have acknowledged that this made them vulnerable to exploitation. In their families of origin, only one of the 12 women observed a father doing any kind of indoor chores. All agreed that they got their standards from their mothers, who were invariably described as pathologically clean. Only one mother 'hated doing housework' and her daughter confessed that she did not notice mess, and her untidiness was a legitimate source of irritation to her partner.

Femininity and housework are closely intertwined in the role-modelling done by mothers, which can elicit quite conflicted responses in their lesbian daughters. Some admire their mothers, feel great compassion for their disadvantage and exploitation, and in some ways seek to emulate them. Others, while absorbing their mothers' standards, are concerned not to share their mothers' position of powerlessness and exploitation. This seems to result in a need to have their partner fully participate in domestic labour, whether or not that is fair in terms of time investment, or even when they acknowledge that their standards may be extreme. Gina, for example, during a period of not being in any paid employment while her partner was working full-time, still expected Rosie to take an equal share in the housework. Jo, on the other hand, had come to an understanding that her standards were excessive, and that she had been too demanding of her partner. Rather than changing her standards, however, she said she was trying to shoulder more of the burden herself.

For many lesbians, the modulation of gender is not so much about the danger of forfeiting a conventionally female identity, which many see as of dubious value in any case. It seems to be more about not inhabiting the conventionally feminine position of subjection. The more 'femme' her gender presentation, the more a woman can increase her 'bass' setting without being seen as too masculine or dominating, whilst the more butch women can dial up their 'treble' without appearing to inhabit that place of female subjugation.

A Fluid Division of Gendered Roles

Thus the study has demonstrated that, despite popular expectations to the contrary, the lesbian and gay couples who participated in this study do not take on heteronormative stereotypes in relation to their intimate relationships. None of the couples displayed the pattern of one taking a conventional male role and one a female role in their approach to the division and practice of domestic labour. Rather than stereotyped 'women's work' and 'men's work,' I identified . . . eight factors that figured prominently in the participants' accounts of how they arrived at those styles. Unlike [Christopher] Carrington [author of *No Place Like Home*], who found that the couples he interviewed colluded to hide any behaviours of either which appeared too gender deviant, I observed a very different dynamic. All the participants demonstrated a clear critique of conventional masculine and feminine gender roles, with no apparent desire to emulate them in any way. In the context of the private space of the home, and in relationship to the individual who was currently their intimate partner, each gay man and lesbian performed both femininity and masculinity by means of how they engaged with domestic labour. The result is a unique gender style for each individual, a style which is continually modulated, negotiated and refined.

"When young kids aren't in school, they don't display much sex segregation."

Children Do Not Naturally Segregate by Sex

Rosalind Barnett and Caryl Rivers

Rosalind Barnett is a senior scientist at Brandeis University in Massachusetts and director of its Community, Families, and Work program. Caryl Rivers is a professor of journalism at Boston University, a columnist, author, and media critic for news agencies across the United States. The following viewpoint is taken from their book Same Difference, *a joint project that examines the limitations on human potential created by stereotypes of gender roles and abilities. In the viewpoint, the authors contend that boys and girls do not naturally segregate by sex.*

As you read, consider the following questions:

1. How does the research of Barrie Thorne expand the understanding of gender and children's behavior, as described by the authors?

2. According to the authors, what differences in children are frequently ignored during observations and study of gender interactions?

3. How do Barnett and Rivers posit that traditional gender roles and expectations for children today affect the lives of adults in the future?

Is there a culture of childhood that, rather than parents, powerfully shapes the nature of children? Do girls and boys inhabit very different and separate worlds and does this separateness create life-long sex differences?

Stanford psychologist Eleanor Maccoby, a pioneer in sex role research, believes this to be the case. "Boys and girls are indeed exposed to two somewhat different cultures," Maccoby says, and she believes that children's identities are often shaped by what she calls "membership in a same-sex collective." . . .

If this sex segregation in early childhood is as pervasive as Maccoby suggests, if inevitable and tenacious gender differences emerge in early childhood and exert their influence throughout life, then there will be grave consequences for us all. Early on, each sex will stereotype the other in ways that make them seem unattractive, strange, and alien to the other. Maccoby believes that the ways kids learn to talk, act, and play in these sex-segregated groups follow them throughout life. What they learn colors their adult heterosexual relationships at home and at work. Maccoby cites solid research for the occurrence of same-sex segregation in childhood, especially in school. The problem arises when she attempts to link children's behavior to the ways adults act, think, and feel. Do we really spend a great deal of time in segregated groups as children? Yes, we do. But as adults, do we behave the way we do *because* of the playing fields of childhood?

Challenging the Data

Can we really draw a direct line between kids' experiences in school and their whole range of adult relationships? This line of thinking ignores the influence of the experiences people have beyond childhood. Maccoby cites only three sources for the idea of the all-determining power of childhood: the very popular but seriously flawed works of Carol Gilligan, Deborah Tannen, and Mary Pipher.... Their work is a slim reed on which to hang so crucial an argument. A much stronger argument for the opposite idea comes from New York University sociologist Kathleen Gerson. She conducted a detailed study of the life histories of young adults and found that the influence of childhood was "underdetermining" when it came to the way their lives evolved. Many other events—their education, the line of work they chose, the bosses they had, the mentors who helped them, the spouses they married—all shaped their lives more powerfully than their early childhood experiences.

Another important question about the culture of childhood is whether sex-segregated play is rooted in our deep species history, as Maccoby claims. Do the boy-girl patterns of play on the school yard reflect styles that date back to prehistory? Probably not, anthropologists say. Our hunter-gatherer ancestors lived for eons in small nomadic groups. In all likelihood there were not many children in any one group, and the children were apt to be of different ages. (The sexes are more likely to separate from each other in same-age groups than in mixed-age groups.) Both sexes most likely mingled freely with each other and the dominant "segregation" was between adults and children, not between boys and girls. We say that with some confidence because we see today that when children are in small groups, they play together without regard for sex. Moreover, in large extended families children tend to segregate by age, not sex: the older kids (or big kids) versus the younger kids (or little kids).

The child's play of our genetic ancestors was likely not "gendered." Toys were probably scarce and created from sticks, stones, or any available material. Children played most often with whatever was around, with no thought about whether it was a "girl thing" or a "boy thing." Our ancestors had no modern advertising to create pink and blue versions of the same toys to promote products for boys and girls.

Studying Children in Natural Environments

So is sex-segregated play natural or created? Eleanor Maccoby seems to opt for the former. But other child developmentalists challenge her view. First, is what we see in school really typical of children's natural behavior, or does it come from a highly structured, rule-bound environment? Barrie Thorne, a highly respected sociologist at the University of California–Berkeley, points out that what science knows about kids comes mainly from only one place—the school yard—where most segregation among children occurs and most developmental research on children takes place—90 percent, according to Thorne.

She approaches the study of childhood differently. She doesn't hone in on school yard behavior but follows kids all day, in many settings, "Start with a sense of the whole rather than with an assumption of . . . separation and difference," argues Thorne. Her work is extremely important because she collected her data by observing kids over long periods of time and she is very sensitive to context. Thorne understands that kids' behavior depends on what kind of school they are in, what kinds of teachers they have, and what activities they engage in; importantly, their behavior varies over time. She doesn't fall into the trap of making generalizations about *all* kids at *all* times.

Thorne reports in her 1994 book, *Gender Play*, that sex segregation only occurs when there are large groups of same-age children supervised publicly by a few adults. In more private and intimate settings, cross-sex play occurs often and easily. And these are the settings in which people spend most of their time—now and in the past. Not until the rise of industrialization were children sent out of the home to school, where there were enough of them to permit sex segregation and where there were few adults charged with their supervision. When you have forty kids playing in a school yard, watched over by one or two teachers, you have to find ways to organize them. Sex is the most obvious category. But it's unlikely that gender was important in determining how kids played back in hunter-gatherer times (roughly 2,000,000–8,000 B.C.), when children played in small groups of kin.

So the segregation we see among school children may itself be an adaptation to an "unnatural" set of circumstances for which humans are genetically ill prepared. That idea goes against the grain, since the tendency is to believe that what happens in school yards is natural. But sex-segregated play may have been created by the institution that was devised to educate children in the most convenient way, *not* by the nature of children themselves. "At school, no one escapes being declared male or female whether that difference is relevant or not," Thorne says. What matters most in the school yard is the way in which children can be easily grouped (boys on the right, girls on the left). In families, on the other hand, parents are most concerned with the individual qualities of their children. In our culture, the model of sisters and brothers offers one of the few powerful images of relatively equal relationships between girls and boys and between adult men and women. The relationships between brothers and sisters begin in childhood, when gender relations in the family are relatively egalitarian.

When young kids aren't in school, they don't display much sex segregation. In neighborhoods, you find a lot more mixing of the sexes than in school. In one neighborhood we know, girls and boys are in and out of each other's houses, they ride bikes together, roller-blade, and shoot hoops together. If there *are* two cultures, they are so fluid that many kids move in and out of them with ease. Even in schools, boys and girls often interact in classrooms, school plays, orchestras, and interest clubs. And a study of how kids behave in a children's museum finds very little segregation between boys and girls.

Adults Treat Male and Female Babies Differently

Starting from birth, mothers attribute different characteristics to male infants than to female infants. Thus, when individual adults are handed the same baby, having been told variously that it is a girl or a boy, *their play, handling of and communication with it differ according to their perception of its sex.* This sort of study shows that babies of different sexes are likely to be treated differently simply because they are of different sexes. A second example makes an additional point. When adults are shown the same video sequence of a child playing, and some are told that it is a boy and others a girl, *their interpretations of its behaviours depend on the sex that they believe it to be.* For example, when the child was startled and believed to be a boy, it was perceived more often as being angry, whereas the same startled behaviour, when believed to be that of a girl, was perceived as fearful distress. This sort of study tells us that expectations about how a male or female baby *should* behave can lead adults to interpret the same behaviour very differently. It raises the possibility that some behaviours may be reinforced or responded to in different gender-specific ways as a result of the expectations of others. Several studies have shown very clearly that the expectations that adults have of a boy differ from those expected of a girl; and men tend to be much more prone to gender stereotyping in this regard than women. Thus, girls are expected to be softer and more vulnerable and are played with more gently. They are also expected to be more vocal and socially interactive, and parents spend more time in these sorts of behaviours with girls. Boys in contrast are encouraged to do things, are less directly communicated with and are disciplined or roughly handled more often.

Martin Johnson and Barry Everitt,
Essential Reproduction, *2007.*

Perceived Gender Differences Overshadow Individual Differences

But the focus on difference between the sexes is so overdone that little attention is paid to "within-sex" difference. Boys often differ more from one another in their temperaments and styles of play than they do from girls. And vice versa. But too many experts ignore this reality and focus only on boy-girl differences. (Also, the situation makes a huge difference. When kids are rollerblading together, for example, their sex doesn't much matter. But when they are trying out for the gymnastics team or the football team, sex makes a big difference.)

When kids are being watched by adults, Thorne notes, boys and girls are more likely to avoid each other. When adults aren't around, kids are more flexible. Their behavior changes when the situation changes—when they're lining up on their own for the cafeteria, trying out for band, or playing spontaneously, boys and girls don't separate. At one elementary school Thorne studied, fifth grader Kevin arrived on the school yard with a ball. Seeing potential action, another boy, Tony, walked over "with interest on his face." Rita and Neera were already standing on the playground nearby. Neera called out, "Okay, me and Rita against you two," as Kevin and Tony moved into position. The handball game began in earnest with serves and returns punctuated by game-related talk—challenges between the opposing teams ("You're out!" "No, exactly on the line.") and supportive comments between team members ("Sorry, Kevin," Tony said when he missed his shot; "That's okay," Kevin replied). The game went on for about five minutes—no evidence of sex segregation here. Then other children began to arrive. One more girl joined Rita and Neera, and three more boys joined Kevin and Tony. One was John, a dominant leader among the boys. Suddenly the game changed from a casual one in which boys and girls happened to be on different sides to a "highly charged sense of girls-against-the boys/boys-against the girls." Each sex started jeering and teasing the other. Finally boys and girls started chasing each other, and that broke up the game.

Why did John's arrival have such a big effect? The other boys didn't want him to see them as sissies, and he encouraged the jeering at the girls. If you happened on the field at that moment, you would see a "snapshot" of highly segregated play. If you'd arrived a few minutes earlier, you'd have seen casual, relaxed mixed-sex play. John is a leader. He's dominant, assertive, and draws attention to himself. He's exactly the kind of boy researchers notice, and therein lies a major problem with the two-cultures model—*who* gets studied. The focus is usually on kids (like John) who behave the way they're expected to—the dominant boys and the passive girls. Kids who don't fit the pattern get ignored. Most boys, for example, aren't "dominant" most of the time. A hierarchy needs a lot of subordinates. Thorne sees "a skew toward the most visible and dominant" that leads to a silencing and marginalization of the majority. She sees a "big man bias" in research on children, which equates the behavior of male elites with "typical" boy behavior. "Other kinds of boys may be mentioned, but not as the core of the gender story." However, more than half of the boys in a classroom she examined intensively did *not* fit into the rigid stereotype of the way boys are supposed to behave.

Defying Gender Expectations

This bias is not limited to research. Many of the popular new books written for parents about how boys get shortchanged in school (e.g., *The War Against Boys* by Christina Hoff Sommers and *The Wonder of Boys* by Michael Gurian) portray only one kind of boy. He's dominant, rough-and-tumble, assertive, fidgety, and rather inarticulate. But many boys are not like that at all. They're not physically aggressive and not sports-minded; they are highly verbal, love to read, and are able to converse on a high level with adults.

In one of the classrooms Thorne observed, she found four boys—Jeremy, Scott, Bill, and Don—whose relationships were exactly like the intimate, sharing modes of connecting that are usually ascribed to girls. "Jeremy, who had a creative imagination, spun fantasy worlds with one boy at a time . . . acting as detectives tracking footprints on the playground. Jeremy and his partner would share treasured objects." The identity of Jeremy's adventuring partner of the moment shifted between the boys via a "breakup" process often claimed to be typical of girls. "The boy on the outs would sometimes sulk and talk about the other two behind their backs." When Scott was excluded, he would activate a long-standing affiliation with Don. When Bill was on the outs, he went solo. "Over the course of the school year I saw each of the shifting pairs, Jeremy and Bill, Jeremy and Scott, Scott and Don—celebrate themselves as 'best buddies.'" The pattern of their relationships, Thorne says, "fit the shifting alliances claimed to typify girls' social relationships, but *boys* were the protagonists." . . .

Childhood Gender Expectations and Adult Behaviors

The bottom line is that that when we all buy into boy-girl innate differences, we're limiting both sexes and, oddly enough, not preparing either sex adequately for the world as it currently exists. When we assume boys won't play with the nurturing and house-care toys—even though research shows they will—we're telling them that nurturing and domestic chores are not part of their future. But if we don't encourage boys to play with the toy vacuum cleaners now, they're going to need five "queer" guys showing them how to play with it when they grow up or risk losing the girl [as happens on the television show, *Queer Eye for the Straight Guy*]. If we don't encourage girls to play competitive sports and learn to "gut it out," they're going to be less prepared to enter a highly competitive workforce that demands that we do indeed "gut it out."

The message being sent by many scientists who study child development is that children are more flexible than some theorists—and much of the popular media—acknowledge or allow. Children are not doomed to one-dimensional lives by the power of mothering, nor by behaviors cemented into their psyches by prehistory, nor by the sex-segregated playgrounds of childhood. Overall, science tells us, much of what we understand as "gender" is a social construct that we ourselves build, rather than something we inherit. Small differences between the sexes are blown out of proportion and take on nearly mythic dimensions. From minutiae like separate toy aisles to color-coded clothing to grand theories of how boys and girls learn and think differently, we have spun an elaborate fantasy about the sexes that is not moored to the solid dock of fact. We are only starting to realize the extent to which this is true. Our own actions and attitudes can indeed change the shape of the world that will be our children's legacy.

> *"The boys and girls produced and af-firmed meanings [of the tale of Cinder-ella] consistent with their gender, and actively worked to ensure these pro-cesses."*

Children Recognize and Reinforce Gender Roles

Lori Baker-Sperry

Lori Baker-Sperry is an associate professor in the Women's Stud-ies Department at Western Illinois University. She has conducted extensive research on how the portrayals of men and women in classic fairy tales influence the perception of gender, culture, and the balance of power between the sexes. The following viewpoint describes how first-grade boys and girls reacted to the images and behaviors of male and female characters in Walt Disney's Cinderella.

As you read, consider the following questions:

1. According to the author, why was Walt Disney's *Cinder-ella* chosen for this research project?

Lori Baker-Sperry, "The Production of Meaning Through Peer Interaction: Children and Walt Disney's *Cinderella*," *Sex Roles: A Journal of Research*, vol. 56, June 2007, pp. 717–27. Copyright © Springer Science & Business Media, LCC 2007. Reproduced with kind permission from Springer Science and Business Media and the author.

2. How does the girls' group's response to *Cinderella* indicate their understanding of traditional gender roles and expectations, according to Baker-Sperry?

3. What group response to *Cinderella* did the boys formulate and how did they control it, in the author's account?

Scholars have identified fairy tales as vehicles of gendered messages and forms of prescriptive literature for children, and others have argued that such gendered messages are interpreted and reinforced through peer interaction. [Sociologist William] Corsaro identified children's literature, particularly fairy tales, as important sources that are "primarily mediated by adults in cultural routines in the family and other settings." The intent of the present study was not to document which messages are gendered, but how gendered messages are understood and internalized by children and, further, the ways that such tales are interpreted through peer interaction. The static, gendered messages and the highly structured form of the fairy tale provide a vehicle for children to interpret gendered norms and expectations more clearly.

The well-known tale *Cinderella* was chosen for its clear, traditional depiction of gendered expectations, fantasy, and romantic love as well as for its current status as a feminine text limited to the world of girls in its recent production and advertisement (e.g., a story central to the "Disney Princesses"). *Cinderella* is a tale that focuses on girls and women, with predominantly female characters. Boys are not likely to embrace a female main character. Girls, however, are often willing to embrace a male main character such the popular children's character, Harry Potter, for example. Choosing *Cinderella* for the present study was an intentional way to clarify the reactions to a book clearly identified as targeting one sex and not the other. The choice of a "feminine" text that illuminates this relationship between boys, girls, and gendered text was deliberate. . . .

Retelling the Tale: A Form of Social Power

The girls in the present study often found social power or acceptance in the retelling of the tale. For the girls, there was more at stake in telling the story as it was read, than in changing the story to reflect less traditional roles and behaviors. This was documented in numerous ways; for example, one girl was quickly admonished by another for suggesting that "maybe Cinderella did not like her fancy ball dress." In keeping with [researchers C.] West and [D.H.] Zimmerman's theory of gender work and performance, the girls wanted to be perceived as feminine and, therefore, to prove their femininity through sharing components of the tale within the peer group. By retelling and defending the tale as it was read, they reinforced their positions as girls and as knowledgeable of the feminine world. Assertion of femininity was most influential with other girls, but the boys did not problematize the girls' interest (as they did with other boys'). These examples lead to questions about the extent to which "doing gender" influences the process of interpretation and the construction of meaning within the peer group. If active negotiation is about sometimes resisting dominant messages in favor of working out meaning within the peer group, but doing gender is about affirming gendered stereotypes within the same group, the two ways of understanding and making sense of the world are at odds. . . .

The Boys in the Group: Peer Culture of Resistance

It should come as no surprise that the boys generally defined *Cinderella* as a "girls' book," and, although often they actively listened or commented, they made it clear from the beginning that this is not the book they would have chosen. This was an expected response based upon the chosen text. Even though there were many loud guffaws at the introduction of the text, it was fairly clear that the boys were as familiar with the tale as the girls were. The boys did answer questions and offer comments, but as often as not it was to steer the discussion off track. This tactic was noticeably common among the boys, and they engaged in some friendly competition as to who might be the most successful, complimenting each other on a job well done.

The boys also rivaled one another for the attention of the group and for my attention. As we had spent time in other forms of classroom interaction, our relationships were often friendly and familiar. But, when it came to approval from the group or my approval, the boys usually sought approval from the group. This was often manifested in raucous storytelling. Their stories or comments interested the group because of their (sometimes sexually suggestive) shock value.

LBS [Lori Baker-Sperry]: On Cinderella's feet were . . ?

Mike: Shoes.

Larry: Glass shoes.

Chorus: Glass slippers!

Larry: It looks like a glass dress!! I wish it were a glass dress!

Larry: Ha! It would be funny if it was . . .

Mike: And then we could see . . .

LBS: All right. Her slippers are the only clothing item made of glass. . . .

The boys did not elaborate on the tale in ways that identified with the prince, the king, or with Cinderella. Furthermore, the boys did not experience any social rewards from other boys for knowing the story. In fact, most of the boys adamantly argued that they did not care for the story at all and reacted negatively toward any boy who showed any sign of interest in the tale. The only boy who took an interest in the prince used a different characterization than what was offered in the tale, although his description clearly resonates with masculine culture and expectations of male sexuality.

Mark: I think the prince has a lot of dances.

Joe: What? Dances?

Mark: He dances and dances and dances because he likes to kiss lots of girls . . .

Joe: Oh, yeah, well he does not dance if he doesn't have to. [shrugs]

Mark: He does have to so he does.

Joe: Yeah, I would dance if I had to.

Mark: What?

This conversation illustrates the tension between the social expectations that the boys sensed from one another and the larger adult world, as well as the conflicted nature of the traditional stories of heterosexual love and masculinity. Examples such as this, when juxtaposed with the preceding examples of some of the girls' responses, demonstrate the reproduction of larger social norms concerning sexuality and desire, as well as acceptable roles and displays for men and women.

The Acceptability of Interest in the Tale

The boys were not always willing to offer a response, presumably for fear of disapproval from the other boys in the group. In one group, for example, I could not elicit a verbal response from any of the boys unless I asked them a direct question, and then I would receive a very short reply. One shrugged his shoulders at a general question aimed at the group; the others shifted sidelong glances at each other. They did not seem to feel the need to feign enthusiasm for the book. A girl in the group stated that the boys did not like it because ". . .it is a *girls'* book, even though there are men in it." . . .

In each of the groups, most of the boys began to disengage within the first 10 minutes. Inevitably, one or two boys began quietly to discuss something other than the story, and the other boys quickly tuned in to what it was that they were doing or saying. In fact, if a boy in the group did not become engaged in these other interests, he was often solicited by a boy sitting next to him, or the other boys would look at each other and signal about him. For example, one boy who seemed to be shunned by the group as a whole engaged neither in conversation about the text nor in the boys' alternate conversations. Most boys ignored him, although one said "Mark likes *Cinderella*" in a derogatory way, to identify Mark as "not one of us." Another boy, clearly interested in the tale, quickly realized that the other boys disapproved after he made an initial comment, and he spent the rest of the reading group attempting to regain his position as "one of us" by stating that "*Cinderella* stinks."

These findings illustrate how gendered behavior is expected of and by boys and girls. Whether Mark had earlier shown an interest in "girls' stuff" or was alienated from the boys as an unpopular student, his gender was suspect and became a means of torment. The second boy is an example of the work commonly done to regulate masculine behavior. Most students were very in-tune with the group's expectations for gendered behavior and quickly accommodated. [Bronwyn] Davies argued [in a 2003 book] that teasing and alienation serve to maintain the categorical boundaries between the constructions of femininity and masculinity. This regular, everyday maintenance work was evidenced here in the boys' treatment of the group member who deviated from the expected response. . . .

The very act of defining the text as a "girls' book" authenticates the assumptions of gender difference for the boys and girls.

Acceptance of *Cinderella*'s Gender Messages

The children's behavior within the reading groups was highly influenced by group interaction. This is in keeping with Corsaro's assertion that most socialization occurs at the level of interaction, be it in the family, among peers, or elsewhere. The nods and sounds of approval from group members encouraged both acceptance of the media messages and interac-

Early Sex-Segregated Peer Relationships

Sex segregation is one of the most powerful and pervasive social phenomena known to exist in childhood. Sex segregation begins around the age of 3 years and escalates over childhood. By the time children enter preschool, young boys and girls show strong and consistent preferences for same-sex peers over other-sex peers. Not only do young children show strong preferences for same-sex peers, they also spend relatively little time with children of the other sex. In particular, children spend very little time solely with members of the other sex. By most estimates, over half of all young children's peer interactions involve play with same-sex peers, about 30% involve mixed-sex peers (playing with both a boy and a girl), and less than 10% of peer interactions involve play only with other-sex peers. With age, the proportion of same-sex peer preferences increases, at least through the elementary school years. For instance, [Stanford University psychologists Eleanor] Maccoby and [Carol Nagy] Jacklin reported that preschoolers were three times as likely to interact with same-sex peers whereas 6 1/2 year olds interacted with same-sex peers 11 times more often than they interacted with other-sex peers. . . .

Richard Fabes, Carol Lynn Martin, and Laura Hanish,
Merrill Palmer Quarterly Journal of Developmental Psychology,
July 2004.

tion and interpretation of those messages, depending upon the perspective of the group. An uncomfortable group atmosphere was often evident in conjunction with "doing gender."

The girls and boys were highly influenced by the group, and acceptance or rejection of the text was enhanced by whether or not the children identified with the story, whether they thought that it was or was not about them. This is no doubt one of the reasons that the boys in the present study did not enjoy the tale, or did not *openly* admit to doing so. *Cinderella* is a text that resonates with social messages aimed toward girls (e.g., social rewards for goodness, kindness, and care as well as an emphasis on feminine beauty) and does not problematize a beauty ideal, romantic love, or competition among women for the attention of men. The messages routinely found in books for boys, such as an emphasis on strength, the ability to protect others, and the denial of emotions, are not prevalent in *Cinderella*.

The girls embraced the story, identified with the female characters, and actively engaged in filtering the text through their lived experience and expectations of the future. They clearly took pleasure, for the most part, in reenacting the fairy tale, taking particular delight in the transformation of a young, downtrodden girl into a beautiful princess. The tale was well known, and well loved, by most of the girls. There were instances, however, when a girl was admonished for wanting to be Cinderella because she was seen by the others as not attractive enough, when the girls discussed ways that their experiences sometimes more closely matched the stepsisters', or occasions when the anxiety produced by the normative expectations of femininity became evident ("How does Cinderella get to be so beautiful?"). But, for the most part, the acceptance was unanimous and excited.

Through the girls' discussion of the story, traditional expectations for femininity were identified, reified, and reinforced. The strong identification with the tale, as evidenced by the girls, is an indication of the social importance of traditional expectations of femininity. In light of previous research that has identified girls as active negotiators in the construction of meaning, the unquestioning response to the traditional elements of the tale signifies the importance of gendered expectations and the solidity of gendered boundaries. The girls responded with a clear reaction: *Cinderella* is about us! Such a reaction, from any single girl, evidenced and affirmed her femininity.

Making Their Own Meaning

Cinderella was not, however, about or for the boys. As a feminine tale, any association might be seen as feminizing for them. This supports a traditional ideology associated with heterosexual masculinity. Furthermore, it might be expected that a boy would respond differently, possibly more positively, outside of the group setting (e.g., at home reading with a parent, or reading on his own) if the expectations to "do gender" were less. Through group displays, the boys demonstrated resistance to the messages in the tale and reinforced group acceptance of normative masculinity. The textual association with romantic love, messages traditionally directed toward women and girls (e.g., domestic work, competition for men, emphasis on beauty), and the packaging of the text (i.e., colors of pink and purple with "cute" animals) inherent in *Cinderella* simply do not mesh with boys' experiences in learning about masculinity or the cultural expectations of them. These conflicts are reinforced through interaction in the peer group, and the peer group often regulated interpretation.

The boys also actively moved the story to a place that was more about them. In this way, they de-centered the central character and instead turned to other components of popular fairy tales that are more interesting to them, such as chasing dragons and engaging in adventurous sword play. They also shifted the focus from the story in general to challenging my authority as its reader. . . . This is in keeping with their quick and decisive treatment of each other when gender boundaries were crossed. Davies identified similar responses in the preschool children she observed. Corsaro's assertions concerning the influence of the peer group on the interpretation and production of meaning were evident in the reading groups conducted for the present study. The children actively participated in peer socialization through the use of encouragement, enticement, pleading, and, sometimes, ridicule. The children dealt with the messages and images together, often building on one another's sentences and nodding in agreement at the final product. At other times, their disagreement contributed to an understanding of the complexities of the questions raised. The boys and girls produced and affirmed meanings consistent with their gender, and actively worked to ensure these processes.

| *"The exclusion of women from playing at the highest level of any sport is cultural rather than physical."*

Women Can Compete Against Men in Sports

Phil Dimitriadis

Phil Dimitriadis teaches literary studies at Victoria University in Australia, where he is researching portrayals of Australian rules football in fiction. Australian rules football, or "footy," is more like rugby than American football. Footy does not break a team into offensive (agile and fast) and defensive (large and strong) players. A female's smaller size, then, is much less of a disadvantage. In the following viewpoint, Dimitriadis explores the argument that it is training and conditioning, not gender differences, that prevent women from playing footy on the same teams as men.

As you read, consider the following questions:

1. Why was Evelyn Rannstrom removed from the Dandenong Rangers Junior Football League, as described by the author?

2. According to the author, what cultural influences affect a woman's decision to play (or avoid) sports?

3. According to journalist Maria Burton-Nelson, as cited by Dimitriadis, why do men emphasize gender differences in sports?

Evelyn Rannstrom is a 14-year-old footy player who took on and defeated the boys on and off the field. She plays for Gembrook Cockatoo under 14s.

The Dandenong Rangers Junior Football League decided she wasn't allowed to play beyond that age group. They thought of 14 as the age where boys become men and girls become women.

Most girls would have meekly accepted the decision and retired gracefully. Not Evelyn. She decided to take legal action and won her right to play the game she loves.

Her courageous stance could set a vital precedent in the way we perceive the role of women in playing our game.

Could a woman line up in an AFL [Australian Football League] side if she proved that she had the necessary skill, athleticism and toughness needed to play the game?

Footy Should Include Men and Women

Sam Mostyn became the AFL's first female commissioner in 2005 (it took the VFL [Victorian Football League]/AFL 108 years to appoint a woman) and, although some cynics may argue the case of tokenism, she is at least in a position where her voice can be heard, even if there are those who feel she will not be respected.

Mostyn recognises the powerful cultural influence of football and is keen to help women establish career paths through the game.

In the [AFL] *Record*, Peter Ryan writes: "Along with the other commissioners, she thinks acknowledging the important role women play in football is important—for the develop-

The Knuckleballer Is a Girl

Eri Yoshida is the first female—and the youngest—professional baseball player in an all-male league in Japan. Even as a lightweight, at 5 ft. (152 cm) and 114 lb. (52 kg), Yoshida pitches a mean right-handed knuckleball—a throw with speeds of about 100 km and an unpredictable trajectory that she says no batter has yet been able to hit. That's the weapon the Kobe 9 Cruise team hopes will lead them to success when the Kansai Independent League starts its first season in April [2009].

Coco Masters, Time, *November 25, 2008.*

ment of the game, for community campaigns relating to women and to ensure football is a welcoming and inclusive environment for all people."

It is interesting to note the use of the word 'important' twice in the one sentence. To what degree is this importance recognised and how far will the AFL and other 'football' codes go to change and accommodate the way women relate to the game?

Only Culture Separates Women Athletes from Men

Former sports journalist and American academic Maria Burton-Nelson, in her book, *The Stronger Women Get the More Men Love Football*, offers a radical view on the subject.

She believes that women should be encouraged to develop their physical capabilities to the point where they can compete with men in the same domain. She argues that the exclusion of women from playing at the highest level of any sport is cultural rather than physical.

She thinks that women are led to believe that they cannot compete against men in these sports at elite levels because body strength and conditioning has been seen as the point of difference in intense male contact sports:

"In fact, few professional athletes have 'natural' bodies; otherwise we'd bump into pro football-sized men in the supermarkets. Women who play or do not play sports have been shaped by various factors, including restricted access to training opportunities, restrictive shoes and clothing, ridicule by peers, and cultural pressure to limit food intake for the sake of creating a thin, rather than strong, body.

"There's nothing natural about any of that. But because sports seem natural, and because in the sports media we so often see men who are bigger and stronger than the biggest, strongest men, these men make a convincing subliminal case."

Burton-Nelson's argument should not be easily dismissed. She focuses on the major issue that prevents women from competing with men, and that is the way gender is a culturally conditioned practice in relation to sport.

In the case of AFL, there is no reason why a woman who follows a similar training regimen to the male players cannot develop the speed or bulk to compete.

Athleticism Has No Gender

This possibility may appear to be light years away, but not that long ago young girls were discouraged from playing any [kind] of football.

Junior football teams now include talented girls up to under 14 years of age and maybe beyond because of Evelyn Rannstrom's stand. AUSKICK [a youth football organization] has become even more popular because girls want to play footy with and against the boys.

Ten years ago this reality would have seemed preposterous, but not any more. Skill, speed and strength are not gender specific, so why should football or any other sport divide talent along gender lines?

According to Burton-Nelson the cultural desire to sexualise females in contrast to male aggression plays a major role in maintaining the status quo in the rules of engagement. She argues:

"To assert that women are really not so different from men disturbs our dualistic, bipolar way of viewing the world. If women can participate fully in an activity, whether that activity is combat or coaching or computer programming, that activity can no longer be used to grant men superior status.

"So when women demonstrate strength, some men respond nervously to the impending power shift. 'Amazons' with 'too much testosterone' threaten the concept of men as meatier, mightier, and as warranting special privilege."

The biological argument regarding women as delicate, because they have breasts, also appears as a convenient myth. Male genitals are just as vulnerable as any other body part, but we don't often hear of the need to protect the testicles at all costs when there is a premiership [championship] to be won.

> *"From 1990 to 1998, the time gap between the women's marathon world record and the men's record increased."*

Women Cannot Compete Against Men in Sports

Amby Burfoot

Amby Burfoot is a former Boston Marathon winner and a member of the Road Runners Club of America Hall of Fame; he is also the recipient of several journalism awards. The following viewpoint originally appeared in Runner's World *magazine, an international publication with an audience of recreational and competitive runners. In it, the author examines the source of the theory that women—despite being much slower than men during sprints and short races—have better endurance and will ultimately overtake men's records in long-distance events.*

As you read, consider the following questions:

1. According to the author, what theory has arisen to explain the excellent performances of women marathon runners?

2. What are some factors that caused women's average running times to slow down, as cited by Burfoot?

3. How do women's speeds compare with men's speeds in races across very long distances?

More women are running longer distances than ever before. Gentlemen, should you watch your backs?

At [the 2005] Los Angeles Marathon and Gate River Run 15-K in Jacksonville, Florida, the best women runners will be given a "head start" over the fastest men. In this battle of the sexes, the first person to reach the finish, woman or man, will win bonus prize money. It's a neat idea—running's equivalent of the famous Billie Jean King versus Bobby Riggs tennis match of 1973. It also raises a familiar but fascinating question: Now that more women are running, are they starting to catch the men?

The debate began in the late 1960s when it was noted that the pioneers of women's marathoning often finished with smiles on their faces. The men were gagging and sagging, but the women were waving to the crowds. Hmmm. In the 1977 U.S. 100-mile Championships, Natalie Cullimore placed second among all finishers. Her time was the fourth fastest ever run by an American of either sex. Hmmm again. And then came the theory that has persisted, through debates, controversies, and numerous articles, to the present day: Women are better endurance athletes than men.

In the early 1990s, I devised a plan to test the theory, or so I thought. *Runner's World* mailed questionnaires to 5,000 subscribers, asking each of them three simple questions: What's your gender? What's your best 5-K time? What's your best marathon time?

Comparing Men and Women's Performances

A total of 2,296 completed questionnaires were returned, 1,707 from men and 589 from women. A statistician friend did the analysis. His finding: On average, the men's marathon performances were 10.71 times slower than their 5-K performances, while women's performances were 10.45 slower. In other words, the women slowed down less. They seemed to have more endurance. Moreover, to quote my friend: "While the difference might seem small, it is in fact very statistically significant because the sample size is so large."

It is here that we encounter for the first time the old chestnut from Mark Twain's autobiography—the line about "lies, damned lies, and statistics." My questionnaire was interesting enough. But my conclusion, based on the statistical results, was pure Swiss cheese. Among the holes: Maybe the testosterone-charged men in my sample started their marathons too fast, then hit the wall. This wouldn't prove anything about women having more endurance, although it might indicate that men have fewer brain cells, as my wife has often told me.

The women-have-more-endurance theory received its 15 minutes of greatest fame in 1992 when the popular "Special Correspondence" section of *Nature* magazine published a letter proposing, through statistical trickery, that women would beat men in the marathon by 1998. Since 1998 has come and gone, we can perform pagan dances on this prediction. Indeed, from 1990 to 1998, the time gap between the women's marathon world record and the men's record increased from 14:16 to 14:42.

Banning Performance Enhancers

Wait a minute. How could women be slowing down? The answer came from one of the most insightful running articles ever written, even though it appeared in a most unlikely place, William F. Buckley's conservative political magazine, *The National Review*. In a lengthy story titled "Track & Battlefield", a Chicago businessman named Steve Sailor and the like-named Steven Seiler, Ph.D., an American physiologist teaching in

Gold Medal Swimming Times at the 2008 Summer Olympics

Event	Men's Times (in minutes)	Women's Times (in minutes)
100m Butterfly	0:50.58	0:56.73
100m Breaststroke	0:58.91	1:05.17
100m Backstroke	0:52.54	0:58.96
100m Freestyle	0:47.21	0:53.12
400m Individual Medley	4:03.84	4:29.25
4 x 100m Freestyle Relay	3:08.24	3:33.76

Taken from: The official Web site of the 2008 Olympic Games, www.beijing2008.cn.

Norway, offered proof positive that women in the 1990s were slowing down at all running distances.

Why? Because random out-of-competition drug testing made its debut in early 1989. And because the Berlin Wall came tumbling down the same year, followed by the breakup of the former Soviet Union. This brought an end to the massive sports systems that had given performance-enhancing drugs to athletes (Note: Women benefit more from steroid drugs, so men's performances didn't suffer as much from the withdrawal of steroids.)

Making Up for Lost Ground?

Happily, in this new century, women are getting faster again, as Paula Radcliffe proved with her incredible 2:15:25 marathon world record in April 2003. With that mighty effort, she lowered the male-female differential in the marathon to just 10 minutes and 30 seconds, far less than it has ever been. But does Radcliffe's great leap forward mean that women distance runners are closing the gap on men? Will they eventually catch and surpass men, particularly at the marathon and ultramarathon distances? The answer: No way.

If you believe that women will catch men, you must pull together both a physiological and a statistical argument. Over the years, many have tried, and all have failed. On the physiological front, the favorite argument has been that women have more body fat than men (true) and can utilize that fat as a fuel better than men can (false).

According to Mark Tarnopolsky, Ph.D., an expert in the field, the current research looks like this: Women (A) burn fat slightly better than men, at least when they haven't eaten recently; and (B) burn simple sugars (sports drinks and gels) better than men; but (C) don't store glycogen as well as men when carbo-loading. By the time you add A and B, then subtract C, you get basically no difference. And women still have to lug around that annoying body fat. For this and other reasons, women have a significantly lower maximum aerobic capacity, on average, than men.

Individual Performances vs. Averages by Gender

A woman could use other physiological strengths to beat a man, of course. She could have more muscle (to move the legs faster) or more hemoglobin (to give the muscles a richer supply of oxygen) or a better running economy (to run more efficiently). However, men have far more muscle-building testosterone and hemoglobin than women, and running economy studies have shown no difference between the genders.

But what about ultradistances? If women have more endurance, they should get closer to men as the distance increases. At most track distances, women trail men by about 10 to 11 percent, but Paula Radcliffe is just 8.4 percent behind Paul Tergat in the marathon. Ultra star Ann Trason has won several 150-mile races outright, and Pam Reed beat the men in the Badwater 135-miler two years in a row. Do women catch up with men if the distance just gets long enough?

No. At the ultradistances, women's times—even Trason's and Reed's—trail men by 15 percent or more. The gap gets bigger as the distance increases. And I even checked the Sri Chinmoy Transcendence 3,100-mile race. That's right: 3,100 miles. The event has been held for eight years in New York City, and the current men's record is 42 days, 13 hours, 24 minutes, and 3 seconds. The female record is 49 days, plus 14:30:54. That's a difference of 16.5 percent.

At this point, we'd be smart to stop fussing over statistics and time differentials. We've come a long way since women first started entering road races in the 1960s. The important thing now is simply that women can run any and all distances they choose. Women don't need to chase men. All they need is the chance to chase their own potential.

Periodical Bibliography

The following articles have been selected to supplement the diverse views presented in this chapter.

Michael Abrams — "The Real Story on Gay Genes," *Discover*, June 5, 2007.

Bruce Bower — "Women Have Hormonal Cues for Baby Cuteness," *ScienceNews*, February 28, 2009.

Cordis News — "Does the Brain Have a Sex?" March 9, 2009.

Economist — "Sex, Shopping, and Thinking Pink: Evolutionary Psychology," August 25, 2007.

Joe Garofoli — "Femme Mentale," *San Francisco Chronicle*, August 6, 2006.

Fred Guterl — "The Truth About Gender," *Newsweek*, March 28, 2005.

Chris Macias — "When It Comes to Tasting and Describing Wine, Women Seem to Have an Edge," *Sacramento (CA) Bee*, March 13, 2009.

Linda Marsa — "He Thinks, She Thinks," *Discover*, July 5, 2008.

Amanda Ripley — "Who Says a Woman Can't Be Einstein?" *Time*, March 7, 2005.

Ellen Ruppel Shell — "For Better or Worse, Sex Chromosomes Are Linked to Human Intelligence," *Discover*, October 24, 2005.

John Tierney — "Personality Tests Show Differences Between Men's, Women's Roles," *San Diego Union-Tribune*, September 18, 2008.

CHAPTER 2

What Are Some Cultural Effects of Male and Female Roles?

Chapter Preface

Perhaps the most famous boyfriend in all of English literature is Romeo Montague, the young wooer of Juliet Capulet who is so filled with love for her that he kills himself when he believes she is dead. William Shakespeare's play *Romeo and Juliet* captures all the passion and turmoil of teenage rebellion and desire. Despite the fact it was written more than four hundred years ago, it still resonates with adolescent audiences today.

Romeo is an interesting fellow. At the beginning of the play, he is hopelessly in love with Rosaline, who does not return his affection. Romeo's male friends encourage him to accompany them to a masked ball to see all the other pretty girls he could be with instead. As his cousin Benvolio puts it, Rosaline will look like a crow compared to all the swans he will meet. His friend Mercutio says—in iambic pentameter— the best way to get back at love for being rough with him is to be rough with it, to preemptively prick love in retaliation before it can hurt him again. He means, of course, that Romeo should collect and break as many hearts as he can and that such predatory pursuits will make him feel better. But what does Romeo do? He forgets all about the icy Rosaline when he sees the beautiful Juliet, whom he marries the very next day.

Much is made in the fields of biology and psychology that males are more promiscuous than females, that males have instincts to spread their seed wherever they can, and that women hunker down and build a nest. In humans, polygamous societies—though not the norm—are well known, but polyandrous societies (in which one woman is mated to multiple men) are very rare. Whereas promiscuity in teenage girls is frequently interpreted as a sign of an absent father or self-destructive tendencies, promiscuity in teenage boys is referred to as "sowing their wild oats" and accepted by many as sexual exploration and vigorous health. It is assumed the most popular boys have had sex with many different girls, an assumption reinforced by portrayals of teenage boys on television and in film. Searching for sex partners is seen as a reasonable pursuit, even a lark, and teenage boys' struggles to find willing partners have been the premise of more than one lighthearted movie.

But is promiscuity really the natural and desired behavior of the typical teenage boy? Do they all really wish to make multiple sexual conquests—to be a "player"? Do they even judge themselves against that standard of male adolescence? It wasn't until 2001 that researchers actually asked any boys how they perceived love and what their relationship goals were; the results were surprising. Bowling Green State University professor Peggy Giordano and her colleagues interviewed more than thirteen hundred high school students about love, sex, feelings, and relationships. The boys expressed the same thoughts and concerns about making commitments, moving too quickly, finding partners, and being friends as the girls did. Less than a quarter of the boys identified with the "player" role. Most boys really, truly love their partners as intensely as their female peers do. They want to make commitments; they probably always have, if Shakespeare is to be believed. So why does this cultural expectation that boys and men only want one thing (which isn't romance) persist? Why does society emphasize one particular aspect of masculinity when few males adopt those behaviors—even when given cultural permission to do so?

The following chapter examines some of the beliefs about what roles men and women are told they should play and what roles they actually do play, and considers some of the social, economic, and political ramifications of maintaining stereotypical gender expectations.

"Recent market research indicates that women ... 35–49 spend more time on online games than any other demographic."

Males and Females Both Embrace Gaming Technology

Aleks Krotoski

Aleks Krotoski is an academic and journalist who writes about and studies technology and interactivity. She writes, podcasts, and blogs for the Guardian *newspaper in the United Kingdom and was named one of the "Top Ten Girl Geeks" by the CNET Web site. In the following viewpoint, she examines women's participation in the gaming industry as players and designers. Krotoski notes that despite the cultural belief that mostly men are playing and designing computer games, gaming has been embraced by women of all ages, and because there are more female designers, game design is evolving to reflect their interests and preferences.*

As you read, consider the following questions:

1. According to the author, how have computer games changed since more women have started to play them?

Aleks Korotoski, "Chicks and Joysticks—an Exploration of Women and Gaming," *ELSPA White Paper*, September 2004, pp. 5–14, 21. © elspa 2004. Reproduced by permission.

2. Why are online casual games (versus elaborate console games) so popular with women aged thirty-five to forty-nine, as explained by the author?

3. How does Krotoski suggest the presence of more female game designers will change the gaming industry?

Women are an important part of the burgeoning business model of the future of the games industry. Developers and publishers are courting the Louis Vuitton purses of the fairer sex, with titles that consider their needs, their desires and their modern, active lifestyles.

Technological advancement has opened the doors for the design and development of software and hardware which appeals to this group of gamers. Manufacturers of alternative gaming technologies like mobile phones have exploited the powers of new computer chips to increase the interactive applications on their hardware that appeal to their female consumers. Internet designers have discovered new gaming revenue streams that attract this group in particular. Out of these considerations has grown a broader player base, which is translating into a strong female games-industry workforce, thus escalating the balance between the sexes in studios and increasing gender-inclusive player styles in their output.

This paper examines the role of women in computer gaming, as an audience and as contributors to the future of interactive entertainment. It will show that women are a mounting force behind the scenes and at the tills, and that their inclusion is ushering in the era of games as a mass market phenomenon. . . .

The Girl Games Movement

While early home consoles proclaimed computer gaming as interactive entertainment for the whole family, slowly the player demographics skewed towards boys. During the decade between 1985–1995, both Sega's and Nintendo's machines attracted huge audiences, primarily male players under the age of 18. The output of gaming companies was simplistic compared to the dynamic products released today; it wasn't until 1995, with the enormous success of Sony's PlayStation and with an older target audience that developers and publishers renewed their interest in making products that appealed to a broader market.

Patricia Flanegan, co-owner of arcade machine makers American Laser Games and Sheri Graner Ray, established games designer, set up HerInteractive in 1995 to create games that particularly appealed to girls. The pair self-published adventure title McKenzie & Co. for the teenage and pre-teen female market and shifted a very respectable 80,000 units. Their relative success in an era when 100,000 units was a best-seller was subsequently dwarfed later that year by the release of one of the most successful titles of that decade: Mattell's Barbie Fashion Designer.

The interactive version of the doll, her friends and her family sold 600,000 copies in the US alone in its first year, proving there was a huge opportunity to sell interactive titles to girls and women. Subsequently, Barbie Fashion Designer became a benchmark for titles across the gaming spectrum, and particularly for the new brand of "pink games" which flooded the market. Out of this gold rush came a number of innovative female-centred and female-owned companies like Purple Moon Interactive, headed by industry luminary Brenda Laurel. Laurel's most successful games, including those in the Rockett series, were some of the top titles to be released in the late 1990s. Their teen magazine–style plots focused on conflicts and resolutions set in contemporary and familiar environments. Rockett and others appealed to the girl gamer, and as she grew older they paved the way for titles attractive to the modern woman. Contemporary girl games companies, like the now-veteran HerInteractive, still produce console and PC software based upon this premise, and, particularly in the US, a teenage female market is blooming. . . .

Gaming and the Modern Woman

As games-savvy girls of the 1990s grew into game-savvy adults, they demanded different titles, and the industry responded by releasing a slew of successful "nurturing" games like Creatures and The Sims. Massively Multiplayer Online Role Playing Games (MMRPGs) like EverQuest and There.com also support enthusiastic female majorities of up to 60%, most of whom are over the age of 30. Many of these titles are viewed as opportunities to examine what draws women to interactive entertainment in order to actively develop for this market.

There's also a loud but proud subculture of women who beat the boys at their own games, including all-girl professional first person shooter teams who take on all comers in titles like Quake and Counter Strike. On the opposite end of the spectrum, women are the number one players of mobile games and online simple-format games like Bejewelled and Mah Jong.

In the decade since Barbie Fashion Designer's release, when the vast majority of titles fell into the categories of shooter and sports simulation, publishers have become aware of the vast array of play styles available and attractive to women over the age of 18.

As a result, games developers are beginning to explore methods of making titles more accessible to girls and women. Plots have developed added depth, self-expression in the games abounds and opportunities for tapping in to the natural social nature of women have been introduced. Controllers and other input devices have become more user-friendly. Dance mats, conga drums and maracas have all been successfully integrated into games for the "party" market appealing to players of both sexes from age 7 to 70. Women are gaming more than ever before, bringing their unique vision to interactive entertainment. . . .

The International Female Consumer Market

Internationally, British women play less than games-dedicated countries like the US, Japan and Korea where 39%, 36.8% and an astounding 65.9% play, respectively. In the US, the steep percentage of female gamers in this market is reflective of the 70 million women with PCs and Internet access in their homes. 53% of PC titles are purchased by women, and the computer games charts of 2003 reflect this, with half of the top ten sellers being part of the female-friendly Sims franchise. Furthermore, 41% of women report having an electronic gaming system in their household, and while they may not be the primary users of this technology, anecdotal evidence suggests that game helplines see a spike in the number of phone calls from adult women during school hours.

77.8% of Japan's general public and 69.2% of women have at least one games machine in their home. The country also has a heavily installed user-base of mobile phone gamers, partly in relation to their well-established networks and low-price data tariffs, where 8.7 million users downloaded and played titles from a vast catalogue in 2003. Further, Japan's online games revenues continue to grow, with 3.43 million subscribers across the available games, and while less than 1% of the female general public currently play them, 25% intend to try them. . . .

The Female Gamer

An area of the games market which has benefited from exploiting the female style is the online casual games market. Titles like Bejeweled, Patience and Find-a-Word, found at sites like Chickstop.com, Yahoo Games and others, are quick-fire and low-commitment. Players can log on and log off at their discretion, when they have the chance or need a break. Recent market research indicates that women between 35–49 spend more time on online games than any other demographic.

Percentage of Men and Women Who Go Online

	% Men	% Women
Online overall	68	66
Age in years		
18–29	80	86
30–49	76	79
50–64	63	66
65 and older	34	21
Education		
No high school diploma	32	27
High school	58	56
Some college	79	79
College grad or graduate degree	89	89
Race		
White	70	67
Hispanic	67	66
Black	50	60
Other	72	66
Parental status		
Parent (of child under 18)	81	80
Non-parent (of child under 18)	61	57

Pew Internet and American Life Project, for all surveys for 2005.
N = 6,403.
Margin of error ± 2%.

TAKEN FROM: Pew Internet and American Life Project, "How Women and Men Use the Internet," December 28, 2005.

This population is one of the least considered, yet they are the most dedicated and have the biggest budgets to spend on technology; they will play single-player and multi-player puzzle-based titles for an average of 2.5 hours per week, often on subscription rates.

Women's game choices also reflect their proclivity to use technology in order to learn new skills or about themselves. For girls, play has always involved an element of practice for a future life of domesticity. According to [Massachusetts Institute of Technology professor and gender studies author] Henry

Jenkins, girls' toys consistently have an explicit aspect of exploration as learning, instead of exploration for the sake of it, which more often reflects boys' toys.

Many of the games that have been released since the early days of the industry are punishingly goal-oriented, emphasising supremacy over the environment, in harsh colours, to repetitive music and consistent with boy-centred themes. Girls have gravitated away from these products allowing boys to dominate the home machines and the arcade boxes. Studies suggest female gamers traditionally adopt software that encourages self-reflection, social interaction and proficiency.

The results of in-depth interviews with 20 women who play games indicate that favourite titles include role-playing games like the Final Fantasy series, narrative adventures like Legend of Zelda, easy-to-pick up driving simulations like Colin McRae Rally, puzzle-adventures like Prince of Persia: Sands of Time, quick-fire arcade puzzlers like Tetris and life simulations like The Sims.

Those who reported that they particularly enjoyed action titles like Halo: Combat Evolved suggested similar reasons for their satisfaction with the game as those who preferred non-action titles.

The presence of a good plot, rich characterisations, choice in how they pursue goals, freedom of self-expression, novelty in challenges, immersion in atmospheric virtual environments, pick-up-and-play capabilities and flexibility.

Women also indicate that identifying with a character is important to their enjoyment of a game. Arguably, as more women have been vocal about their game playing, there has been an increase in strong female protagonists.

However, the presence of so many contemporary titles in this list suggests that modern designers are increasingly incorporating gender-inclusive aspects in their game designs, and that women are eager to respond.

Technological advancements over the past decade have offered developers the computer capabilities necessary to create software that features a variety of game styles within one title, both online and off. This "genre convergence" offers both genders something to enjoy within the same gaming experience, and the broadening demographic indicates that they are succeeding. . . .

Future Research

Increasingly women are turning to interactive entertainment for social interaction, learning and leisure. They, in turn, are encouraging their younger counterparts to continue exploring virtual dimensions, try on virtual skins, and solve real-world challenges in virtual space beyond adolescent boundaries.

The greater depth of story and character demanded by girl gamers is increasingly feasible as entertainment technology continues to advance, offering greater hardware memory and faster processing speeds. Encouragingly, the gap between titles that appeal to both women and men is diminishing, and both categories of gamers are now exposed to a wider variety of gameplay options, experiences and avenues. This has a beneficial impact upon the creativity of the games development community, whose products are increasingly winning battles for popularity against other traditional forms of media, and are finding their ways into previously unlikely cultural avenues, including garnering accolades for design and innovation.

The convergence of multiple forms of media, from the internet to mobile phone technology is also attracting women to gaming, resulting in positive experiences with interactive entertainment, thus driving them to explore alternative options for electronic pastimes. The products that greet them in their pursuits are encouraging them to stay and play.

Furthermore, by including more women in the design process of games, the titles that are being released onto the market are more diverse, attract a wider audience and offer undiscovered kinds of participation. The industry recognises the contributions made by its female employees and happily encourages them to become involved in the innovative, imaginative and exciting realm of game development. Women in the industry are encouraged to reach out to girls and other women and talk about their experiences in one of the fastest growing and most creative industries in the world today. Diversity in gaming can only be positive, for everyone.

"Men look for linearity, formality and a not too colourful look while women look for more colour, more informality and less linearity."

Males and Females Respond Differently to Technology

Gloria Moss, Interviewed by Chris Lake

Chris Lake is an editor at E-Consultancy, an online resource for digital commerce, marketing advice, and insight. Gloria Moss, a senior research fellow in the Business School at Glamorgan University in the United Kingdom, conducts research on how nationality and gender influence graphic, product, and Web design, especially from a human resources perspective. The following viewpoint is an interview by Lake with Moss about how the gender of the Web site designer influences whether men or women will find the Web site more appealing and whether that affects the outcome of an online experience, particularly shopping.

As you read, consider the following questions:

1. According to Moss, what is the "self-selecting phenomenon" of Web site design?

2. As cited by Moss, what factor might make it difficult to teach male Web site designers to create sites that appeal to women (or vice versa)?

3. How can the look of a Web site influence the success of an online retail endeavor, according to Moss?

Chris Lake: *You've recently conducted some research into the importance of gender in web design, which seems to have been pretty much ignored as a subject. What prompted you to conduct such a study?*

Gloria Moss: Several things. For many years, I have been researching men and women's design aesthetics, examining what I call their production and their preference aesthetics. All of this started about ten years ago when I made the surprise discovery that all the paintings I preferred in an exhibition of paintings by men and women were in fact produced by women.

I wanted to get to the bottom of whether this was a chance event, related perhaps to my quirky tastes, or whether this was a more general phenomenon that would apply to other men and women. It did not take long to discover that no one else had published anything on this topic, so the only way to get an answer was to do the research yourself.

I used some pretty rigorous statistical techniques and published the results in papers from 1995 to 2002. These showed that there was strong statistical evidence of differences between the production and preference aesthetics of men and women. My focus up to that point had been graphic and product design, and what the results showed was that—in terms of production aesthetic—there were significant differences in the way men and women used colour, shape, detailing and thematic material.

In terms of preferences, there was a very significant tendency, statistically speaking, for each sex to prefer designs produced by people of their own sex. I called this phenomenon the 'self-selecting phenomenon.'

It made sense to extend the study into the field of web design for two reasons. Firstly, men and women are moving to a position of parity in terms of web usage, and increasing proportions of women are now engaging in e-commerce. It became essential to understand whether the preferences of men and women in terms of web design were similar or different. As you rightly say, nobody had done this research before.

What methodology did you use? What did you seek to find out?

The selection of an appropriate methodology has been key in all of this work, and I was very fortunate in the web design work to have Dr. Rod Gunn, mathematician and statistician, as co-researcher. We did four things.

Firstly, we established whether the production aesthetics of men and women in the UK differed, and if they did, in which ways. Secondly, we looked to see whether these differences went across national boundaries, examining websites in France and Poland as well. Thirdly, we measured the aesthetics used in different industry websites, from beauty websites, with a predominantly female target market, to university websites with a market consisting equally of men and women. Last but by no means least, we measured the preference aesthetics of men and women. . . .

The results? In the UK, 13 out of the 23 features showed up as significantly different between the male and female websites, and twelve emerged as significant when the results of all three countries were pooled. We were fortunate in doing this work with a Polish marketing expert, Krzysztof Kubacki, who analysed the Polish websites. The results showed that the gender differences crossed national borders.

Gender and Age Analysis of Social Networking Users: Social Network Sites

Social network	Gender	Age groups						
		14–17	18–24	25–34	35–44	45–54	55–64	65+
Classmates	Women	142,757	599,895	724,253	240,863	117,584	41,578	10,152
	Men	62,885	278,908	435,742	211,079	100,527	41,874	12,527
	Unspecified	2,532	9,355	9,363	5,346	2,811	1,323	407
Facebook	Women	784,214	1,685,029	767,619	184,057	72,743	21,441	10,270
	Men	357,017	977,753	609,655	177,662	62,033	22,024	8,545
	Unspecified	29,495	82,958	47,769	13,403	4,595	1,549	405
Flickr	Women	87,720	303,941	363,220	139,090	60,707	19,871	5,113
	Men	44,170	235,015	398,061	205,631	89,587	33,994	8,998
	Unspecified	5,163	23,806	25,753	10,982	4,825	1,926	524
LinkedIn	Women	3,697	39,594	178,550	69,197	24,368	7,726	1,355
	Men	4,618	42,642	222,431	124,759	45,310	16,083	3,379
	Unspecified	610	7,905	27,858	13,456	5,264	2,005	402
Myspace	Women	5,158,453	7,091,214	3,800,542	1,252,287	542,694	167,087	71,531
	Men	3,365,442	5,226,788	3,238,471	1,209,510	475,566	167,101	66,852
	Unspecified	3,147	4,726	2,540	1,137	548	251	67

TAKEN FROM: "Rapleaf Reveals Gender and Age Data of Social Network Users" (Press Release), Rapleaf, Inc., July 29, 2008. business.rapleaf.com.

A subsequent step was to measure the extent to which certain industry-sector websites used the masculine or female web aesthetic, and this was done by rating a random sample of websites against the twelve or so features that emerged as significant, and ascribing them a 'gender coefficient.' In all cases, the overwhelming majority of websites emerged as being rooted within a masculine design paradigm.

Finally, in order to compare male and female preferences, a mixture of male and female students (67 in all) were asked to rate a number of male and female-produced websites. It was an exciting moment when the results of this test emerged. What they demonstrated was an extremely strong tendency towards own-sex preference, with men rating the male-produced sites much more highly than the females, and vice versa for the females. In statistical terms, in fact, the effect could not have been stronger.

Assessing Web Design by Gender

In the offline world we know that men and women shop in different ways, whether zigzagging supermarket aisles or responding to colourful product displays, so it follows that perceptions of web design also differ. What do the genders look for in a good website?

Quite different things really. Men look for linearity, formality and a not too colourful look while women look for more colour, more informality and less linearity. The language they use is also different, and the sites women create also have more links than the men's.

From the evidence of the men and women's sites across three countries, it is quite clear that men and women part company on many different features!. . .

Your study suggests that male web designers predominantly design for men. Can you elaborate? Do women design for women? Any ideas on the ratio of male to female web designers? Can men learn to design for women, and vice versa?

People have a tendency to design what they find appealing so in that sense, men will tend to design in the male aesthetic and that will tend to appeal most to men. I have carried out several surveys of the web design industry in the UK, and have consistently found that men constitute about 74–78% of designers.

Can they be taught to design for women? That is a difficult question since it presupposes some understanding of the reasons for the differences. If you assume that the differences are rooted in society and the way that boys and girls are socialised, then you could expect that the differences could in fact be taught.

If, however, you assume the differences to have some sort of biological origin (which I believe has an influence together with socialisation), then it might be more difficult.

Are web designers being taught to consider gender? If not, then I guess this is a big part of the problem.

All this work on gender and aesthetics is pretty new, so only the most enterprising colleges will be teaching it. It is important that these findings are passed on to next generation of designers. At the moment, I imagine that the notion of parallel design paradigms is not a hot topic although nothing would give me greater pleasure than to be proved wrong!

Audience's Gender Should Drive Design

The research seems to prove that there is no one-stop shop approach to web design. So presumably you are suggesting that web design needs to begin with a close look at a prospective target audience, as much as anything?

Absolutely. Our preference tests show clearly that what appeals to one group may be wide of the mark for the other. So, information on the gender constituency of the target market is therefore essential to successful web design.

Let me give you an example. Women are the main market for beauty websites and yet the majority of these sites are designed using a male-production aesthetic. Lots of straight line, boxes, serious images and few colours. From a design point of view, they are not having the impact on their target market that they could have.

How important are the visual aspects of a website in driving e-commerce? Is 'look and feel' as vital as, say, intuitive navigation?

The literature emphasises the centrality of non-price mechanisms of differentiation and the fact that the perceived visual attractiveness and content of the website can influence perceptions as to the site's usefulness, enjoyment, ease-of-use and satisfaction. Relevant factors are likely to relate to technical issues (e.g., speed of loading), content or form.

Where the visual element is concerned, graphics is listed as one of the factors causing dissatisfaction with users in the US and the Netherlands, leading human computer interaction (HCI) specialists to attempt to understand the elements (visual and content) in web design that are valued and those that currently produce a deficit between expectations and experience.

There are analogies with traditional retailing where the form and content of store atmospherics has become an established field of research study. There is wide acceptance of the importance of the retail environment and physical form of a product in creating certain effects in buyers. Where products are concerned, research shows that products perceived as pleasurable are preferred and used more often than those not perceived as pleasurable, leading to enhanced purchasing.

You analysed 300 UK retailers and found that they are very masculine-focused, yet we know that e-commerce is fairly evenly split between men and women. How big is the potential upside, if gender-orientated e-tailers redesigned their sites for men/ women?

The upside is potentially massive. At the moment, the vast majority of websites are employing a single type of aesthetic (the male production aesthetic) and completely ignoring the existence of another type of aesthetic (the female production aesthetic). The same applies in many areas of graphic and product design as well. It is a bit like restricting yourself to a diet of carrots and potatoes. If you didn't know that apricots and carrots existed, that would be one thing. But once you knew of their existence, you'd be crazy to ignore them wouldn't you?. . .

Gender Preferences Transcend Nationality

Despite all the talk of cultural differences across Europe, your studies seem to prove that men and women act in a similar fashion whether in Poland, France or the UK.

Absolutely. We've a paper coming out in the *International Journal of Applied Marketing* that shows this. I had the good fortune of working with a Polish marketing expert, Krzysztof Kubacki, and he sources and analysed the Polish websites.

I've previously compared persuasive design to one of those kid's books with multiple choice endings. What are your thoughts on persuasion, and how can design influence the customer journey to achieve business goals?

That's a nice analogy. I agree with you that one needs to be humble and put oneself in the shoes of the user. All the research I have done over a ten-year period persuades me that the designs people produce are mirror images or X-rays of themselves, and people will respond most positively in the presence of designs that offer them images of themselves.

Let me explain. There is a whole body of work in the field of art therapy and psychology that analyses mood and personality from the colours and shapes that people draw. From this you can perhaps see that people's graphic productions are X-ray images of themselves. There is even work showing that 9 times out of ten, when asked to draw a person, most people will draw someone of their own gender. What we draw is, in many ways, a version of ourselves.

When it comes to selecting a design we like, there is a lot of research that tells us that we select something to express ourselves. In design terms, that means that the product must express a language of colours, shapes and themes that is the visual equivalent of the personalities of the target market.

This is perhaps a new idea to many designers and marketers—that there is a language of graphic expression that can be learned and applied. I have come to perceive this largely because I trained and practised for many years as a human resources professional and was fascinated by projective tests. I learned then that art therapists could encode someone's character from the shapes and colours used in their doodles and paintings. From there to commercial products is just a short step, but one that can radically impact on profitability.

"*Significant percentages of Americans are not giving truthful answers when asked whether they would support a female presidential candidate.*"

The United States Is Not Ready for a Female President

Matthew J. Streb, Barbara Burrell, Brian Frederick, and Michael A. Genovese

Matthew J. Streb is an associate professor in the Department of Political Science at Northern Illinois University (NIU). His co-authors of the following viewpoint, Professor Barbara Burrell and doctoral candidate Brian Frederick, are also members of the Political Science Department at NIU; coauthor Michael A. Genovese is a professor of political science at Loyola Marymount University in Los Angeles. In the following viewpoint they report on the results of a nontraditional poll taken in 2008, which indicate that far fewer Americans are ready to have a female president than traditional polls indicate. The authors suggest that poll responders are unwilling to express honest answers that go against the "correct" popular opinion, and thus responses to the question are often skewed.

Matthew J. Streb, Barbara Burrell, Brian Frederick, and Michael A. Genovese, "Social Desirability Effects and Support for a Female American President," *Public Opinion Quarterly*, vol. 72, Spring 2008, pp. 76–89. Copyright © 2008 Oxford University Press. Reproduced by permission of the publisher and the authors.

As you read, consider the following questions:

1. As cited by the authors, why do respondents to polls often provide misleading or incorrect answers about their opinions?

2. How does a "list experiment" differ in structure from a traditional poll or survey, according to the authors?

3. How do the results of a list experiment about participants' likelihood of voting for a female candidate for president differ from poll responses on the same topic, as explained by the authors?

Public opinion polls consistently show that an overwhelming percentage of Americans say they would vote for a qualified female presidential candidate. These results would indicate that female candidates such as [Hillary] Clinton or [Condoleezza] Rice will not be at a disadvantage in a presidential election because of their sex. Or do they? There is a long line of research showing that survey respondents lie when they believe their true answer goes against perceived societal norms. In other words, people provide the socially desirable response to questions dealing with controversial issues. Traditional public opinion polls are not equipped to tease out whether people are hiding their true feelings on surveys.

Here, we employ an unobtrusive technique that is becoming increasingly popular among political scientists: the list experiment. We hypothesize that significant percentages of Americans are not giving truthful answers when asked whether they would support a female presidential candidate. We find that roughly 26 percent of the public is "angry or upset" by a female president. Moreover, this level of dissatisfaction is consistent across several demographic groups. . . .

Support for Female Presidential Candidates

In 1937, seventeen years after women obtained the vote, and at a time when only a very few women had been elected to public office primarily to temporarily replace their husbands, George Gallup thought to ask a national sample of the American public if they would vote for a woman for president. Asked "would you vote for a woman for president if she were qualified in every other respect," 33 percent responded affirmatively. Since the latter part of the 1940s, Gallup has periodically asked the public "if your party nominated a woman for president, would you vote for her if she were qualified for the job?" The General Social Survey also asked the same question in a series of polls between 1972 and 1998. The number of people who state they would vote for a qualified female presidential candidate from their party has grown steadily. A 2005 Gallup poll finds that 92 percent of the public answered "yes." Similar results exist in another Gallup question that does not specifically ask whether the respondent would support a female presidential candidate from *their* party. When asked, "would you, personally, vote for a qualified woman for president, or not?" 86 percent of the public said they would. However, not everyone is convinced that the playing field has been completely leveled for women in presidential politics. A [2004] study by [Jennifer] Lawless finds evidence that in the aftermath of the 9-11 attacks, voters now express less confidence in women to handle national defense issues which may translate into less support for a female president. Nevertheless, the overriding trends in public opinion data point to greater receptivity on the part of the US public toward the idea of supporting a woman as president.

Social-Desirability Effects on Surveys

The preceding evidence indicates that the United States might indeed be ready for a female president. However, the possibility of people hiding their true preferences on surveys is a constant worry for pollsters. It is not so much a concern that people are giving untruthful responses purposely to distort the findings of a survey (as newspaper columnist Mike Royko once suggested they do regarding exit polls), but that they are not giving honest answers to conform with societal norms and not be embarrassed by their responses. Indeed, there is a long line of research that indicates that participants provide socially acceptable responses to survey questions. For instance, studies find that people say they voted when in fact they did not or say they voted for the winner when they did not. It is also common for respondents to overreport church attendance. . . .

Furthermore, preelection survey questions on vote choice confirm the social desirability hypothesis. The 1989 Virginia governor's race featured African-American Douglas Wilder and his white opponent Marshall Coleman. Wilder led Coleman by a wide margin for much of the campaign but only ended up winning narrowly. A week prior to the election the *Washington Post* released a poll indicating Wilder held a commanding 15 point lead, and two days before the vote was held a *Richmond Times Dispatch* poll showed Wilder ahead of Coleman 45 percent to 36 percent. Nevertheless, the actual results revealed that Wilder barely defeated Coleman, 50.1 percent to 49.8 percent, the closest margin ever in a Virginia gubernatorial election. Many analysts suggested that some white voters may not have been truthful with survey interviewers about their feelings toward Wilder because they felt social pressure to support a black candidate. . . .

[Massachusetts Institute of Technology professor Adam] Berinsky comes to a similar conclusion regarding the 1989 New York City mayoral election between Democrat David Dinkins and Republican Rudolph Giuliani. Dinkins had a sizable lead over Giuliani just days before the election, but won by less than two percentage points. According to Berinsky, this shift in voting occurred because Giuliani voters did not express their support for the Republican candidate for fear of being perceived as anti-black (Dinkins is African American);

instead, many respondents hid their true preferences in the preelection surveys and answered "don't know."

While issues of race may be the most susceptible to social desirability problems, evidence shows that issues related to gender are not immune. Interviewer effects also exist based on the sex of the interviewer. For example, male respondents offer significantly different answers to male and female interviewers on questions dealing with gender inequality in employment. We contend that social desirability effects are found in questions about voting for a female presidential candidate. Because respondents will want to avoid appearing sexist, they will not express their true feelings about a female candidate, saying they would support one when in fact they would not. Evidence indicates that this claim might be true. While 86 percent of respondents in a recent Gallup poll answered that they would vote for a "qualified woman for president," 34 percent said that "most of my neighbors" would not vote for a female president. This result could be a sign that people are "hiding behind" their neighbors instead of stating their true preferences.

The List Experiment

We cannot know for sure whether the neighbor question is evidence of social desirability. After all, it is certainly plausible that 34 percent of people really do believe that their neighbors would not vote for a female president regardless of what their own views are on the subject. Fortunately, there is a much better measure to tease out whether people are telling the truth when asked if they would support a female president. We employ an unobtrusive measure called the "list experiment," which allows us to get a more accurate picture of Americans' true feelings about the prospect of a female president. The list experiment is certainly not new to political science. Scholars have used the list experiment to determine whether social desirability effects exist regarding race and religion.

To conduct the list experiment we obtain two random samples of people. The first group (the baseline group) is asked *how many* of the following four statements make them "angry or upset."

1. The way gasoline prices keep going up.

2. Professional athletes getting million dollar-plus salaries.

3. Requiring seat belts to be used when driving.

4. Large corporations polluting the environment.

The second group (the test group) is given a fifth statement:

5. A woman serving as president.

Again, notice that respondents are asked to tell us only *how many* of the statements make them "angry or upset," not *which ones*. This eliminates the respondent's concern about giving the socially desirable answer and allows the person to reply more honestly. . . .

The Findings of the List Experiment

The results clearly show evidence of social desirability. Traditional polls find anywhere from about 5 percent to 15 percent of the public who say they will not vote for a female presidential candidate, but our results indicate that a significant percentage of people are hiding their true feelings on women president questions. Roughly 26 percent of the respondents expressed anger over a female president, about a 10 percent to 20 percent difference between what traditional public opinion polls indicate. . . .

Anger toward a female president is consistent across several groups, although no statistically significant differences exist between demographics within those groups (e.g., men versus women, south versus nonsouth). Equal percentages of males and females are upset about a female president, a result

Why Has America Not Elected a Female President?

While about 90 percent of Americans say they could support a female presidential candidate, that figure may be deceptive—only about 60 percent said yes when Gallup pollsters asked the more revealing question: Are Americans ready to elect a female president?

"I think we do still suffer from the notion that women are not as good as men—that they aren't as rational. If you have 1 in 10 admitting that to pollsters, you must understand there are still more who think so privately but won't say so publicly," said Farida Jalalzai, assistant professor of political science at the University of Missouri–St. Louis. . . .

Female candidates face a special burden in U.S. presidential elections because the country stands with the largest nuclear arsenal and as the planet's sole superpower. As Laura Liswood, co-founder of the White House Project and the Council of Women World Leaders, has observed, this puts a premium on perceived military expertise. The role of commander in chief conjures up a "warrior image"—one favoring traditional masculinity instead of political instincts that seem more maternal.

What's more, the peculiarities of our American character make it harder for female contenders. In our movie idols and our presidents, Americans value rugged individualism, bravado, a cowboy mystique—a role that men find easier to play, even those who were Ivy League frat boy cheerleaders.

Vicki Haddock,
San Francisco Chronicle, April 29, 2007.

that should be disturbing to people who believe that females should be more supportive of female candidates. Regarding education, more than 23 percent of those without a bachelor's degree and more than 26 percent with at least a bachelor's degree are angered by a female president. . . .

There are also significant percentages of people upset about a female president based on different household income levels. Only for those respondents whose household family income is in the $25,000–$49,999 category did we not find a statistically significant difference between the means of the baseline and test groups. For all other income groups large percentages of people are upset by the prospect of a female president (between 26.78 percent and 29.31 percent). . . .

Significant Evidence

We find significant evidence of social desirability when it comes to answering questions about support for a female president, and it may be the case that the results are even stronger than they appear. We purposely set the bar high to test for social desirability effects by using the same phrase ("angry or upset") as previous research that used the list experiment. We could have used the phrases "concerned" or "opposed" and found even larger differences in the means between the baseline and test groups. . . .

Furthermore, while we used five statements in the test group to help combat ceiling effects, it is possible that they still exist to an extent. Roughly 12 percent of the respondents in the test group answered "four" when asked how many of the statements made them angry or upset. By answering "five," they would not be able to conceal their feelings about a female president. Therefore, it is likely that the number of people who are angry about a female president is actually a few percentage points higher than what our findings suggest.

We believe the findings have implications both regarding the future of women in political office and the accuracy of public opinion polls. First, while women candidates seem to be making some strides in races for many offices including executive positions like governor, the office of the presidency still may be out of reach. Even as other countries, including Germany and Chile, have elected their first female heads of government, the United States may not do so any time soon. It may be a positive that societal norms regarding a female president seem to be changing. The fact that people apparently no longer feel comfortable giving their true preferences about a female president could be seen as a sign of progress; unfortunately that progress is occurring slowly. On the other hand, simply because citizens are more hesitant to express hostility toward a woman president does not mean this sentiment will translate as readily when they privately cast their ballots. Previous assertions that if qualified women were to emerge as viable presidential candidates they would not face large pockets of discrimination among the electorate need to be reassessed. Moreover . . . , even if a small fraction of the population is resistant to the idea of voting for a woman president this fact could still tip the balance against the female candidate in a close election. Given that the number is much higher than the traditional surveys indicate, there is reason to think that aspiring female presidential contenders have a steeper hill to climb than many observers believe.

Equally disturbing is that this opposition is consistent across numerous groups of people. Some of the demographic groups that have been documented as most supportive of women candidates in public opinion polls appear to be concealing their unease toward a woman in the White House. Just as liberals are less likely to support affirmative action than they claim in traditional surveys, women, younger people and the highly educated are less sympathetic to the idea of a female president when the pressure to conform to social norms is not heightened.

Second, we certainly are not implying that polls are always wrong and that they cannot measure people's true opinions. On most issues most of the time, scientifically conducted polls are extremely accurate. But this paper is another in a long line of research that suggests that when the question deals with a sensitive issue, those findings must be approached with caution. There is a natural tendency for individuals to express opinions that are congruent with the norm of gender equality. Polls asking whether a respondent is willing to vote for a woman president are likely to produce artificially high levels of support simply because many persons do not wish to be seen as possessing attitudes that are discriminatory toward women.

| "While Americans perceive this country to be on the cutting edge of, well, everything, the world is already waaayyy ahead of us this time."

The United States Is Ready for a Female President

Elayne Boosler

Elayne Boosler is a comedian and an animal rights advocate and rescuer who hosts a blog at The Huffington Post, *an online newspaper that covers news and provides analysis on topics ranging from politics to entertainment, the media, and the environment. In the following viewpoint, written a year before Hillary Clinton became a serious candidate for the 2008 presidential election, it chides Americans for believing they live in a country that leads the world in society and culture when in actuality many other nations have already elected female heads of state.*

As you read, consider the following questions:

1. Why does the author point out that having a female Speaker of the House during President George W. Bush's second term was an important milestone only in the United States?

Elayne Boosler, "'Is America Ready for a Woman President?' Go to Hell," *The Huffington Post*, February 2, 2007. Reproduced by permission.

2. Why does the author consider the question of whether the United States is "ready" for a female president insulting?

3. Why does the author criticize the idea that people like to elect as president candidates with whom they'd like to share a beer?

Two years to go until the [2008] presidential election, and it boggles my mind how many times I've already seen this sentence: "Is America ready for a woman president?" That's usually followed by some stuff about how much you would like to have a beer with the candidate being a predictor of electability. Maybe this question keeps being written by some of the 79% of Americans who don't have passports, because here's a flash: while Americans perceive this country to be on the cutting edge of, well, everything, the world is already waaayyy ahead of us this time.

While Americans clapped wildly at the last State of the Union address when George W. Bush said he was making history with these words, "Madame Speaker," it was only American history. Sixty-seven years earlier, in 1940, Khertek Anchimaa-Toka was the Head of State of Tannu Tuva, which then joined the Soviet Union in 1944. She continued in various government positions until 1972. No word on how many people wanted to have a vodka with her.

A Global Trend

In 2007, a record 13 countries have currently serving, elected female Presidents or Prime Ministers: Ireland, New Zealand, Latvia, Finland, The Philippines, Bangladesh, Mozambique, Iberia, Chile, Jamaica, South Korea, Switzerland, and a Chancellor in Germany. None have renowned ballet companies, or have ever asked neighboring countries if their maps make them look fat. All play some kick-ass soccer.

Will Japan Ever Let Women Take the Throne?

In the absence of guarantees that there will be more male heirs coming after Prince Hisahito, the imperial succession will be far from stable.

The only group of people who still insist that only males can claim the throne are conservatives and former court nobles who were stripped of their status after World War II but who still maintain informal ties with the imperial family.

Most Japanese do not seem to care whether it is a male or female on the Chrysanthemum Throne and are, in fact, all in favour of opening up the job to a woman.

The question of whether succession should be thrown open to either sex will be raised again before too long.

Kwan Weng Kin, Asia News, January 23–29, 2009.

In 2002, the list was also at a record 13, with Sri Lanka, Indonesia, Panama, Senegal, and Sao Tome and Principe replacing some of the above, with only one of them being flooded by God.

Add to those, these countries, which elected female Presidents as far back as 1980: Iceland, Malta, Nicaragua, and Guyana. American TV shows debuting in 1980 included *Bosom Buddies*, where two men played women, *It's a Living*, about spunky waitresses with a surprising amount of cleavage for a non-Hooters hotel dining room, and *Too Close for Comfort*, about a father who meddled in the lives of his grown daughters, who lived in the apartment downstairs.

Countries with female Prime Ministers, some as far back as 1960 include: Sri Lanka, India, Israel, Central African Republic, United Kingdom, Dominica, Norway, Yugoslavia, Pakistan, Bangladesh, Poland, and Turkey. The only power available to American woman in the 1960s was Flower Power.

Countries with interim female Presidents as far back as 1953 include; Bolivia, Guinea-Bissau, Haiti, East Germany, Liberia, Ecuador, Georgia, and Mongolia (Chairman). In America in 1953, some of the top movies were; *Gentlemen Prefer Blondes, How to Marry a Millionaire, Calamity Jane, The Farmer Takes a Wife,* and *Peter Pan.*

Many of these women were also re-elected, for example in Norway, where the female Prime Minister served from 1981–86, 1989, and 1990–96. For three years running, the United Nations has ranked Norway the number one place in the world to live (based on standard of living, life expectancy, education, democracy, public health). Norway's economy is based on oil and gas, mining, shipbuilding, fishing, paper products. Mary Kay Cosmetics overtook none of those industries.

In Pakistan, Prime Minister Benazir Bhutto was the first woman to head the government of an Islamic state. She served from 1988–90, and 1993–96. Before being elected, she spent almost six years in prison or under detention for her political activism. She was ousted twice in corruption scandals, which may or may not have been political witch-hunts, but hey, that's as good as the men. Too bad Muslims don't drink, I'd sure like to have a beer with her. [Bhutto was assassinated later in 2007 while campaigning for office.]

These countries have had acting or interim female Prime Ministers as far back as 1979: Portugal, Lithuania, France, Burundi, Canada, Rwanda, Bulgaria, Guyana, Mongolia, Finland, Peru, Macedonia, and Ukraine. In America in 1979, Bo Derek was elected the country's number one sex symbol for her role in the movie *Ten.*

It's All in the Phrasing

When people write, "Is America ready for a female president?" they need to know how insulting that is to women. These are the doubt planters. Tell 'em to go to hell. They're not asking, they're undermining. If you want to make someone feel unwell, don't say, "You look terrible," because he'll immediately bounce back with, "I feel fine!" But if you ASK, if you say, "Do you feel all right?" the doubt sets right in. "Why? Why do you ask? What's wrong?" That's what they're doing. "Is America READY for a woman president?" "Why? What's going to happen??"

Is America ready? The rest of the world probably reads that and shakes its head in bemusement, or incredulity, plain confusion, or maybe even sadness. Is America ready for sliced bread, covered wagons, indoor plumbing, math, the wheel, air travel, computers? Duh. You're so cute.

A word about the beer thing. I remember the "pundits" saying over and over again during the [2004] presidential election that everybody wanted to have a beer with George Bush but not John Kerry. Well, they should have had a beer with Bush, and elected John Kerry. How did this suddenly become the benchmark of electability? I don't want a president I'd want to have a beer with. I want someone so busy, brilliant, and sterling that I would be terrified to have a beer with her. I want her way too busy, and way too smart and serious for me. I want her having her beers with presidents, prime ministers, scientists, philosophers, and heads of state. But guys, if you can't get past it? Then vote for the woman you'd most like to get drunk.

Periodical Bibliography

The following articles have been selected to supplement the diverse views presented in this chapter.

Alison Avery et al. — "America's Changing Attitudes Toward Homosexuality, Civil Unions, and Same-Gender Marriage, 1977–2004," *Social Work*, January 2007.

Andrew Bahemuka — "Women Left Out of the Land Equation," *Africa News Service*, February 23, 2009.

Keith D. Ciani, Jessica J. Summers, and Matthew A. Easter — "Gender Differences in Academic Entitlement Among College Students," *Journal of Genetic Psychology*, December 2008.

Martha M. Lauzen, David M. Dozier, and Nora Horan — "Constructing Gender Stereotypes Through Social Roles in Prime-Time Television," *Journal of Broadcasting and Electronic Media*, June 2008.

Sarah Tsing Loh — "Should Women Rule?" *Atlantic*, November 2008.

Patrick May — "More Laid-Off Men Means More Mommy Breadwinners," *San Jose (CA) Mercury News*, February 17, 2009.

Bill Pitts — "Women, Ministry, and Identity: Establishing Female Deacons at First Baptist Church, Waco, Texas," *Baptist History and Heritage*, Winter 2007.

Helen Rees and Jan M. Moyes — "Mobile Telephones, Computers, and the Internet: Sex Differences in Adolescents' Use and Attitudes," *CyberPsychology and Behavior*, June 2007.

Nancy Shute — "The Trouble with Boys: What Parents Can Do," *U.S. News & World Report*, September 15, 2008.

**OPPOSING VIEWPOINTS® SERIES**

CHAPTER 3

How Do Gender Stereotypes Affect Perceptions of Men and Women?

Chapter Preface

The Harry Potter franchise is one of the most successful literary endeavors in publishing history. The series of seven young-adult novels chronicling the adventures of the adolescent wizard Harry Potter has been made into successful Hollywood films and has been accompanied by companion texts, fan stories, and dozens of online communities. The author, J.K. Rowling, is a multimillionaire and a global celebrity and has been formally commended by the Queen of England. She was a first-time author when *Harry Potter and the Philosopher's Stone* debuted (published in the United States as *Harry Potter and the Sorcerer's Stone*); the publisher decided to print the books with the initials J.K. Rowling rather than her full name, Joanne Kathleen Rowling. Why? They wanted the books to be popular with young boys and feared boys wouldn't read adventure stories written by a woman, even with a male protagonist.

It is an old story. Throughout history, women have published anonymously or under male pseudonyms, and not always just to appeal to a male market—sometimes just to get a publisher to even read their manuscripts. Men, too, have published under female pseudonyms when the subject matter of their books—such as romance novels—fit into the "women's books" category. Publishing companies often opt to avoid alienating potential readers by offering the "wrong" author for the topic. For whatever reason, women make up the bulk of romance novel readers, and they demand women authors. How much, the unspecified, generic (female) romance novel reader wonders, could a man author know about being a woman in love and finding the perfect man? Alternately, how much, the unspecified, generic (male) sea-adventure story reader wants to know, could a woman author know about piloting a ship in the eighteenth century?

The questions of how much femininity is required to understand being in love and how many twenty-first-century writers of either sex know anything about piloting ships two hundred years ago are never asked.

Men interested in golf would take seriously a nonfiction book about golf written by professional golf champion Lorena Ochoa; women read relationship advice books all the time that have been written by men. Factual information can be explained by members of one sex to members of the opposite sex with no loss of audience. In the realms of fiction associated with men or women, however, readers often seek out authorities of their own sex and reject the work of the other—even when the story is exactly the same.

Writers are of course not the only professionals saddled with expectations of gender-appropriate knowledge and behavior. Many women select female doctors not because the thought of being treated by a man makes them uncomfortable but because they don't believe a male doctor could understand their health. Many male bodybuilders work with male trainers because they don't think a female trainer would be strong enough to help them with the heavier weights. Male child-care workers are sometimes distrusted by parents; women soldiers have been a source of controversy for decades. For some fields, the biological sex of the practitioner trumps any knowledge, skills, and experience a person has worked hard to acquire, and he or she is punished by potential clients merely for an accident of birth.

Some individuals facing this kind of sex disapproval and/or discrimination are inspired to work twice as hard to prove they can excel in whatever roles they choose. Other people give up at the thought of how much effort would be required to overcome social resistance and find something else to do. The luckiest ones pursue their courses of action, encounter obstacles and often overcome them, work as the only man or woman in a group, and don't worry about it further. The following chapter looks at some of the gender biases and stereotypes that still dictate how men and women should behave and tells the stories of how men and women have capitulated to or defied them.

> "Real-life families have changed considerably since 'Mr. Mom' appeared, with more men sharing child-rearing and household chores."

Stay-At-Home Dads Are Reversing Stereotypes

Marilyn Gardner

Marilyn Gardner is a writer and frequent contributor to The Christian Science Monitor. *The following viewpoint discusses the rise in stay-at-home dads in recent years. Gardner addresses and confronts the societal view of a bumbling stay-at-home dad. Although media poke fun at the stay-at-home dad and present a laughable image, men are finding stay-at-home parenting rewarding and nothing like the clichéd, superficial stereotypes.*

As you read, consider the following questions:

1. What movies help to enforce the bumbling father stereotype, according to Gardner?

2. What is a benefit of portraying stay-at-home dads as humorously inept, the author's opinion?

3. What effect do the stereotypes and comedic portrayals of stay-at-home dads have on women, in Gardner's view?

When screenwriters and authors portray men as full-time fathers, many follow a simple rule: Play it for laughs. It has been 20 years since the movie "Mr. Mom" regaled audiences with a stay-at-home dad named Jack, who bumbled his way through diapers, discipline, and such domestic terrors as a runaway vacuum and an overflowing washer. Now Jack's 21st-century counterparts are arriving, and similar humor prevails. The movie "Daddy Day Care" open[ed in May 2003], starring Eddie Murphy as an unemployed father who starts a "guy-run" day-care center with a buddy. The "Mr. Mom" formula remains firmly in place: Men + kids = laughs galore.

That theme also runs through two new books by at-home fathers. In both, Dad cares for the kids while Mom works to support the family. Publishers describe these books as "hilarious." Producers use the same adjective for "Daddy Day Care," along with "sidesplitting."

Demeaning Portrayals

Real-life families have changed considerably since "Mr. Mom" appeared, with more men sharing child-rearing and household chores. But public portrayals often remain stuck in stereotypes of hapless domesticated dads. That image rankles some men in real-life role reversals, who think the laugh-track approach demeans what they do.

"It's almost as though the media want us to think of them as bumbling fathers, but they're not," says Peter Baylies, founder of the At-Home Dad Network.

A report released [in May 2003] by the Council on Contemporary Families finds that American men do more housework and child care than men in any of the other four developed countries surveyed: France, Italy, Germany, and Japan.

Finding humor in parenthood is nothing new, of course. Erma Bombeck played motherhood for a million laughs. And as Scott Coltrane, a professor of sociology at the University of California, Riverside notes, "Comic, inept dads have been around for a long time."

In the late 1970s and early 1980s, a number of "househusband" books were published, many written by reporters taking a year off. "There's now kind of a genre for the new dad: the involved, nurturing father, celebrating the joys of actually being a parent," he says.

Popular culture both honors and makes fun of men in families, Professor Coltrane says. "Cultural images feed off men's and women's anxieties over changing gender and parenting roles."

He describes "contradictory tensions" in cultural stereotypes. "In one, men are bumbling idiots—they can't do anything. In the other, men are capable, nurturing, caring, and loving people. Both are addressed to women. One makes women feel good because he's a bozo and can't do it. The other is more a wish fulfillment that there actually are men out there who are kind, caring, sensitive, even sexy."

Ironically, Coltrane adds, "Men are lampooned when they're doing more."

David Eddie, author of "Housebroken: Confessions of a Stay-at-Home Dad" (Riverhead, $14), playfully calls himself "Cinderfella" and a "faceless drudge." He takes his toddler son to his favorite watering hole with him, and leaves him at a lingerie shop called Nearly Naked, in the care of the owner, a friend, while he runs errands.

Similarly, in "I Sleep at Red Lights: A True Story of Life After Triplets" (St. Martin's). Bruce Stockler describes himself as "an anomaly, like a mermaid or an anarchist." The stay-at-home dad, he writes ruefully, is "a socially awkward reality in the suburbs." Yet, ever the humorist, he goes for laughs as he describes taking his three young sons and daughter to the ladies' room at a shopping mall, because it was cleaner than the men's room.

Humor Helps Acceptance

Mr. Baylies speculates that humor in these movies and books helps to counter deep ambivalence about role reversals. "The real changes in families might not be what the public wants to hear," he says. "Maybe we're afraid to lose the notion that moms aren't always going to stay home. There's always that masculinity thing that Dad wants to hold on to, that macho image. It's hard to give up. It's so ingrained in us. I don't think the public wants to let it go. But it's happening gradually."

Baylies, of North Andover, Mass., sees heartening signs of progress, from changing tables in McDonald's men's rooms to play groups for at-home fathers and their children. He has cared for the couple's two sons, now 11 and 8, since he was laid off as a software engineer in 1992. His wife teaches school.

One self-described househusband in southern California, a former lawyer who wants to be identified only as Mark, has been home with the couple's three sons for nearly 10 years. He calls entertainment-media images of men like himself "clichéd" and "superficial," adding, "There is depth to what we're doing."

In American society, he says, "there's not much left in terms of what it's OK to poke fun at. Jokes about women, ethnic groups, and gays are frowned on. But men at home remain fair game."

Still, he remains hopeful that as more men assume new roles, "we will eventually reach a crossover point where it won't be that funny anymore."

The Number of Stay-at-Home Dads in the U.S. Is Rising Dramatically

Year	Number of stay-at-home dads	Percent change from previous year	Number of stay-at-home moms	Percent change from previous year
2002	105,000	—	5,200,000	—
2003	98,000	−6.7%	5,388,000	+3.6%
2004	147,000	+50%	5,571,000	+3.4%
2005	142,000	−3.4%	5,584,000	>+1%
2006	159,000	+12%	5,646,000	+1%
Total change	154,000 more dads at home	+51.4%	446,000 more moms at home	+8.6%

TAKEN FROM: Data Compiled from the U.S. Census Bureau. www.census.gov.

Being A Stay-At-Home Parent Is Rewarding

As fictional househusbands and real-life at-home fathers grapple with doubts, fears, and guilt about their unconventional roles, they also find themselves redeemed by family life. The eternal verities of parenthood bring satisfaction: It's hard work, but it's rewarding, too.

No wonder these "sidesplitting" movies and "hilarious" books specialize in heartwarming endings. "I look upon taking care of him as a crucial step in my spiritual path, in my development as a human being," Mr. Eddie writes.

Echoing that theme, Mr. Stockler says, "I love my children fiercely."

Mark, too, finds unexpected rewards. "You're an easy target for ridicule, but you're also an easy target for people to praise you and tell you you're great," he says. "What I do is no different from what mothers have always done. But I get a lot more credit."

> "Male and female parents bring differ-
> ent qualities to their roles, but it would
> be iniquitous to suppose there was an
> automatic difference in their commit-
> ment."

Fatherhood Is Not Valued in Society

Ruth Wishart

*Ruth Wishart is one of Scotland's leading journalists. She has
held senior editorial positions at the* Scotsman, Sunday Mail
and Sunday Standard. *She currently writes a weekly column for
the* Herald *and presents the "Values Added" program for British
Broadcasting Corporation Radio Scotland. In the following viewpoint, she notes how men's abilities and rights to make decisions
about being fathers have been devalued by cultural assumptions
and societal customs. Wishart also explores some recent court
cases that support men in their efforts to be respected as parents
equal to mothers.*

As you read, consider the following questions:

1. What victory did Howard Johnston win in the case brought to court by Natallie Evans, as discussed by Wishart?

2. According to the author, how did the case of Diane Blood differ from the case of Natallie Evans?

3. As the author shows, what message is sent to soldiers who are fathers when society laments the danger facing mothers who are soldiers but not those confronting fathers in combat?

Have you noticed people never use the phrase "fatherhood and apple pie"? How they talk about parents and parenting when they really mean mothers and mothering? We are strolling in the foothills of the 21st century and yet our notional stereotypes of the male/female roles seem preserved in some kind of stubborn, sociological aspic [gelatin].

When women fulminate, quite properly, about the inequalities dished out to the female sex in terms of employment, pay and career advancement, maybe we should also take a hard look at how little we value men's capacity to nurture, and how that may impact on the value systems within the workplace.

When we complain that it is so rarely men who pick up the tab for sick kids, their care and their essential health-related appointments, perhaps we could take time to examine how much we casually denigrate their capacity to fulfill these parental roles with competency. That it is a man's world in terms of material reward and advancement is still a hard statistical fact of life, but only the willfully blind cannot see that today's young fathers inhabit a different planet from their fathers and entire solar system from their grandfathers.

Fathers Unfairly Blamed for Parenting Failures

In the largest federally funded study ever undertaken on the subject [of parental abandonment], Arizona State University psychologist Sanford Braver demonstrated that few married fathers voluntarily leave their children. Braver found that overwhelmingly it is mothers, not fathers, who are walking away from marriages. Moreover, most of these women do so not with legal grounds such as abuse or adultery but for reasons such as "not feeling loved or appreciated." The forcibly divorced fathers were also found to pay virtually all child support when they are employed and when they are permitted to see the children they have allegedly abandoned.

Stephen Baskerville, Independent Review, *Spring 2004.*

Fatherhood Is Rightfully a Choice

There is a strength in male gentleness that we too often ignore or belittle. Examine two stories which much exercised the media [on April 10, 2007]. One was the extremely sad case of Natallie Evans, who failed in her final throw of the legal dice in the Grand Chamber of the European Court of Human Rights. Natallie and her former partner [Howard Johnston] stored frozen embryos when they learned she had cancer and would likely become infertile, which she now has.

Subsequently, they split up and Howard Johnston refused to give her permission to use the embryos, as is his right under UK laws on IVF [in-vitro fertilization], which require both parties to agree to implantation. This is surely classic confirmation that hard cases make bad law. Of course, it must be intensely painful to cope both with childlessness and the knowledge that the possible means to remedy that are within your physical but not your legal grasp. But the embryos were created by a couple and belong to a couple. Mr. Johnston's continuing ability to procreate with another partner rubs salt into the gaping wound of her frustration, but it cannot alter the fact that any child she had would have Mr. Johnston as its natural birth father.

Those of us opposed to forcing women who become pregnant accidentally to give birth regardless of their wishes would find it hard, in logic, to deny men the same rights to choose. Self evidently, being pregnant and giving birth are quintessentially different experiences from contributing sperm and largely becoming a spectator for the next nine months.

But in an age when we have given children born through IVF the right to have full knowledge of their natural parentage, that opportunity denies men the anonymity previously guaranteed in sperm donation. Additionally, what does it say about our view of fatherhood if we consider Mr. Johnston's wishes so irrelevant that we are wholly insensitive to his concerns about having his genetic progeny born in defiance of his express wishes?

In truth, there have been no winners in this six-year battle to resolve the increasingly bitter conflict between two people who were once close enough to consider spending the rest of their lives together. She proclaimed herself "distraught," he "crumpled with relief." Both have been emotionally battered. The previous case of Diane Blood, who successfully petitioned European courts to have two children using the donated sperm of her dead husband differs in the important respect that he could no longer be affected by the decision. Then there was the televised interview with Leading Seaman Faye Turney [who was among the British military detained by Iranian military in 2007], during which it was alleged her captors had told her failure to comply would lead to her never again seeing her little daughter.

Men Are Not Expendable Parents

No account I've read appeared to feature the family circumstances of most of her [Turney's] male colleagues or whether or not they, too, feared being separated from their children. Equally, the only persistent questioning she encountered from the blessed Sir Trevor [the television interviewer] concerned the advisability of young mothers being in the front line. Young fathers, by comparison, were implicitly expendable. Male and female parents bring different qualities to their roles, but it would be iniquitous to suppose there was an automatic difference in their commitment. And counterproductive to continue to suppose that, in some indefinable way, a mother will always give a superior brand of care.

When paternal leave, brief as it is, was first mooted [debated], it attracted widespread derision, as if there was little need for a father to have an early bonding experience with his new baby. OK, the dads aren't much in the breastfeeding department, but cuddles and kisses are gender neutral.

> *"It is not surprising that women are se-*
> *duced too by the stream of media, video*
> *games, patriotism, and valorization of*
> *the most destructive aspects of mascu-*
> *line culture."*

Women Are Not Recognized as Military Heroes

Jennie Ruby

Jennie Ruby is a feminist writer and staff member of Off Our Backs, *a feminist journal in Washington, D.C. The following viewpoint addresses whether women can be as aggressive as men in combat. Ruby presents the problems of women becoming as aggressive as men, but also notes that women need to be more involved in combat and leadership roles. Ruby concludes that the ultimate goal should be to strive for a world without aggression, instead of focusing on achieving combat equality.*

As you read, consider the following questions:

1. As cited by the author, what are some reasons people list for the lack of women in combat roles within the military?

2. According to Ruby, what are some problems with women becoming more like men?

3. What media has culture used to glorify aggression and violence, in the author's opinion?

In an era when women hold almost every conceivable job, where women are heads of nations, captains of industry, astronauts, and surgeons, there is one area where our culture is still reluctant to admit women: to combat roles in the military. Women are just not as aggressive, women don't have the strength, or even "we're just not ready for that" are some of the arguments against admitting women to these jobs.

Can women be as aggressive as men in combat? The question calls to mind one asked by Henry Higgins in [the 1960s film] *My Fair Lady*, Why can't a woman be more like a man? Well, the answer is, no doubt, that she can. But the real question is, do we really want her to be?

There are two ways this latter question ends up being answered: First, traditional conservatives answer no—they do not want to see women be more like men. They want to preserve an ideal femininity, in which women are pure and nurturing and motherly, while also preserving traditional masculinity, and thus maintain the power dynamic of male dominance. Second, feminists for whom the main goal of feminism is equality between the sexes answer yes. They give the automatic answer that of course women can and should do anything men can do. The result is a long string of women firsts; the first woman astronaut, the first woman enrolled in West Point, and so on: women doing men's jobs and taking on male roles. All of which seems to be a good thing, until you realize that the pursuit of equality goes only one way: women are spending a lot of time trying to be like men, and vice versa? Not so much. Yes, there are more stay-at-home dads, there is more room for men to care for children and change diapers today than 30 years ago. But at the core our society wants to hang on to some extreme preserves of masculinity.

Both of these answers, women should be traditionally "feminine," or, women can do anything men can do, leave out the real question.

Unanticipated Side Effects

The problem with women becoming more like men, more equal, in a society that has always been male dominant and male centric is that there may be an unanticipated and perverse side effect: that the society's entire cultural compass will become skewed toward the masculine. As women are absorbed more and more into the formerly male areas where the most extreme forms and characteristics of masculinity are valued, there is a net increase in people who practice violence, machismo, aggression, competition. So in moving toward equality we need not to ask whether a woman can do everything a man can do—but we need to ask, should a woman do everything men do and, more importantly, should anyone—male or female—be doing those things? We recently had our first woman serial killer. Do we want even more women to move in that direction, to achieve equality? Obviously not. In fact, if men could move more toward equality with women on this particular valence, and move their rates of committing serial murder closer to zero, that would be a tremendous benefit to society. From a feminist perspective, we need to step back and take a wider view. What we really should be doing is forging a common ground where we decide what activities we want humans to do, to be involved in, to value—and then work toward equality in those areas. Equal access to projects that are fundamentally antithetical to feminism, to life, and to the planet should not be a platform that feminists spend much time rallying around.

Where Have All the Strong Women Gone?

If the symbol of 1930s Hollywood was Bette Davis in *Jezebel* defiantly wearing red to her virgin-white ball, today it is Cameron Diaz in *There's Something About Mary* rubbing semen into her hair because she is too dumb to realize it's not hair gel.

As women have progressed, the women we idolize—in the movies, on television—have dramatically regressed. . . .

The few strong women in Hollywood movies and TV are safely located in an unreal world: Buffy the Vampire Slayer, Xena: Warrior Princess. The closest to an unapologetic feminist is Lisa Simpson—and she is eight years old, and a cartoon. This isn't because Hollywood is especially sexist. Hollywood largely gives us what we want—and we don't want to idolize strong, powerful women today.

Johann Hari, Independent *(London), March 27, 2008.*

Women in the Military

On the question of women in the military, one feminist solution is that yes, we need women to be involved in every aspect of it from top to bottom, including combat roles and leadership roles and even the role of commander in chief. But what do we want that military to do and be capable of and be used for? That is where feminist values need really to come into play. That is where cultural change needs to happen.

Conservatives profess to be shocked to see women taking an aggressive role in combat, women coming home from Iraq with amputations and other severe combat wounds, and women coming home in body bags. But from a feminist point of view, we should be just as shocked and saddened to see boys and men, any human beings, doing and experiencing these things. And on the individual level we are. But culturally, the extreme forms of aggression and violence committed and experienced in the military are not only accepted for men but glorified in movies, books and songs. It is not surprising that women are seduced too by the stream of media, video games, patriotism, and valorization of the most destructive aspects of masculine culture.

But let's not lose sight of what we really want: a world without military. A world without aggression. A world where no mother's child has to come back dead in order for justice and freedom to be preserved. If we keep this goal clearly in mind, then we can examine how to begin to get there from here.

> *"Women are increasingly finding themselves on the front lines, and their heroics in the face of danger are being recognized."*

Women Are Recognized as Military Heroes

Laura Yao

Laura Yao is currently a staff writer for the Washington Post *but was interning at the* Pittsburgh Post-Gazette *when the following viewpoint was originally published. In it, Yao examines the increase in the number of military women serving in Iraq and the related increase in the number of medals these women are being awarded. Private First Class Stephanie McCulley—a medic who dragged an injured man to safety and saved his life—is just one of many female soldiers who have been honored as war heroes for their brave deeds and military accomplishments.*

As you read, consider the following questions:

1. As related by Yao, why did Pfc. Stephanie McCulley ignore her training and risk hostile fire by rushing back to her convoy after it had been attacked?

2. According to the author, why are so many female soldiers ending up in combat despite rules that prevent them from fighting on the front lines of a battle?

3. As described by Yao, what controversy surrounds the U.S. Army's distribution of medals to male and female soldiers?

On May 8, Private First Class (Pfc.) Stephanie McCulley was traveling in a convoy in Iraq when shrapnel from a roadside bomb struck one of the Humvees. Two soldiers in the vehicle were killed and a third was injured.

Pfc. McCulley, a Uniontown [Pennsylvania] native and Army combat medic, rushed to the aid of the wounded soldier, ignoring the risk of hostile fire, and ultimately saved his life.

"I had been trained to wait for the casualty to be brought to me, but I knew that if anyone was alive, I had to get to them fast," said Pfc. McCulley, in an e-mail sent from Iraq. "We are like a family, and these guys are like my brothers. Losing two of them is the worst pain that I have ever felt."

For her valor and service, Pfc. McCulley received a Bronze Star on June 1 [2007], joining the ranks of the multitudes of women who have played a role in America's military history—from those who acted as spies and nurses to those who dressed like men in order to join in the fighting.

Not the War They Trained For

In Iraq, however, the terms have changed. More women have enlisted in Iraq than in any other war in U.S. history—as of the end of April [2007], 82,000 had served in Iraq or Afghanistan, about 11 percent of the total Army contribution. And in a battle with no discernible front lines, waged in a country with no guarantees, women like Pfc. McCulley are being drawn into the fighting in a way that the United States government never intended.

"The way that we fight here makes it difficult to determine who the enemy is," she said. "The enemy is not dressed for war; the enemy is camouflaged as a local."

"She didn't go in expecting heavy combat," said John McCulley, Pfc. McCulley's husband.

But heavy combat is unavoidable, and women are unavoidably involved. Despite the Pentagon's policy of banning women from direct combat, female soldiers are facing the same risks as males.

"We are all on the front lines ... they are just not drawn as clearly as they were in the past," wrote Pfc. McCulley. "We are the ones who react to enemy contact, who pick up the pieces of our fallen soldiers and continue to fight."

Judy Madison, director of the U.S. Army Women's Museum, attributed this to the type of war that soldiers are fighting in Iraq.

"We're putting more women where it's possible for them to be exposed," she said.

Lt. Col. Kevin Arata of U.S. Army Human Resources Command agreed.

"We're facing a different form of warfare than we were five or 10 years ago," he said. "The front of the war is everywhere, and women are seeing more combat experience."

Women Recognized for Valor and Duty

What's more, women are earning recognition for their contributions. As the number of women fighting and performing valorous acts increases, so too does the number of honors they earn.

"More women are winning medals because more women in the service are in harm's way," said Lt. Col. Arata.

The Army does not keep official records on how many women, specifically, have won awards, but those who have won battlefield honors have entered the national consciousness to a greater degree than ever before.

Queen of England Awards the First Military Cross to a Female Soldier

Private Michelle "Chuck" Norris, 19, had only recently completed her Army training when she braved heavy sniper fire to climb on top of a Warrior armoured vehicle to haul her sergeant to safety after he was wounded in the head.

One bullet from an AK47 rifle ripped through her rucksack as she came under fire from five different positions. But she refused to let go of Colour Sgt Ian Page, dragging him to safety and then jokingly referring to him as "Dad" as they and their comrades waited in the darkness for a rescue helicopter.

The details of that terrifying mission in Al-Amarah were still running through her mind as she received her Military Cross during an investiture with the Queen.

Nigel Bunyan,
Telegraph (London), *March 23, 2007.*

"If you have more women who are enlisted, more are going to receive commendations," said Robin Dexter, the archivist at the Army Women's Museum in Fort Lee, VA. But it only seems like they are earning honors at a higher rate than before because "it's much more public now."

In 2003, national attention focused on Jessica Lynch, who was awarded a Bronze Star and a Purple Heart after being captured by Iraqi forces. Lori Ann Piestewa, who died during the same attack in which Pfc. Lynch was captured, was awarded a Purple Heart. And Sgt. Leigh Ann Hester became famous as the first woman since World War II to earn a Silver Star, and the first ever to earn it for close-quarters combat.

Participants in an Old Tradition

The deeds for which these women won awards builds on a trend that began in World War II. As women no longer serve solely as support staff, they no longer solely win awards for bravery in nursing wounded soldiers.

The only woman ever to win the Medal of Honor, for example, was Dr. Mary Walker, a surgeon during the Civil War. In 1917, Congress revoked her medal in order to make the award more prestigious, but Dr. Walker continued to wear it until her death. President Jimmy Carter restored the honor posthumously.

"Through the time of Dr. Mary Walker to World War I, it was nursing," said Ms. Dexter. But as World War II began and the Women's Army Corps was incorporated, "there are citations for nurses, but also for women serving on the Signal Corps and Multi-Level Security."

Army Stingy with Medals

Despite the public attention on women who have received awards, the Army has still received criticism for being too stingy with its medals, regardless of gender.

Army records show that in World War II, 301 Medals of Honor were awarded; during Operation Iraqi Freedom, there has been only one. In January 2006, a story on CBS ran with the title, "Where are the medals for troops in Iraq?"

In February 2004, however, an MSNBC story, "Is the U.S. Giving Out Too Many Medals?" quoted Col. Jack Jacobs, who received the Medal of Honor, saying, "It's an age-old problem with the Army . . . the authority to approve most awards is at a very low level, and that has a tendency to increase their frequency."

Controversy over medals aside, some facts remain: Women are increasingly finding themselves on the front lines, and their heroics in the face of danger are being recognized in the public arena.

A Sense of Accomplishment

Pfc. McCulley is a perfect example. She was en route to a local sheiks' meeting when the blast killed two members of her patrol. With no regard for her own safety, she left her armored vehicle to treat the third casualty.

"When I talk to him now and know that he is alive because of what we did, I feel a great sense of accomplishment and pride," she said.

Pfc. McCulley's family now lives in Fort Benning, Ga., where she is stationed. She will be in Iraq until June 2008, but, said Mr. McCulley, "The colonel she works for is old school. He makes sure she calls, so I get to talk to her at least twice a week."

According to Mr. McCulley, Pfc. McCulley had always wanted to join the military.

And even though it meant she would have to be away from her husband and two sons, ages 2 and 3, her convictions won out.

"It took a couple of years to convince me, but she talked me into it," he said. "She's a firm believer in helping people who can't help themselves. She believes in what they're doing over there."

"*Men, on average, are willing to devote more time to their career [than women are]*."

Men Are More Successful Because They Make Their Careers a Priority

Marty Nemko

Marty Nemko is an expert career coach and educator who has received attention from a variety of news media organizations, from The Today Show *and* 20/20 *to* The New York Times *and* Los Angeles Times. *He is currently a contributing editor to* U.S. News & World Report *and a columnist at www.kiplinger.com. In the following viewpoint, Nemko addresses the difficult question of whether female corporate leaders can be as successful as their male counterparts.*

As you read, consider the following questions:

1. According to the author of the book *Why Men Earn More*, as cited by Nemko, why do male employees bring home larger salaries than women?

Marty Nemko, "The Real Reason So Few Women Are in the Boardroom," MartyNemko .com, 2009. © Marty Nemko 2004–2009. Reproduced by permission.

2. According to the author, how does splitting time between work and family affect a person's competitiveness as an employee?

3. What effect does a corporate leader's attitude about work have on a company's culture, as described by Nemko?

On average, women are rated as slightly better managers than men. Also, women better understand the female consumer's mindset. That's important because women make most purchases. So why are only 11% of Fortune-500 senior executives women?

The standard answer is "glass ceiling," a term that evokes the image of a cabal of top male executives scheming to preserve an old boy's club.

While vestiges of old-boy hiring may remain, most top executives at Fortune 500 companies are too worried about the bottom line to let any clubby cravings affect who they hire as senior executives.

The primary reason for the 11% figure is that men, on average, are willing to devote more time to their career. And time it takes. A study conducted by The Business Roundtable, an association of CEOs [chief executive officers], found that the average CEO works 58 hours per week. Fortune 500 CEOs likely work even more.

Men at Work

Unlike in typical media portrayals, few male senior executives spend much time hang-gliding. In the real world, here's how it more often plays out, as reported to me by my many clients who are male senior executives. Their exercise is more likely to be on a treadmill while doing professional reading. If he's married, when his wife urges him to do more of the domestic chores and parenting, he is likely to say something like, "I want to rise to the top and you want me to, too. I like my work and you like our lifestyle. That requires lots of evenings and weekends. I spend as much time with the family as I can."

Most women make different choices. The October 10, 2004, lead story on *60 Minutes* and the September 2003 *New York Times Magazine* story documented that a majority even of Ivy- and Stanford-educated female alumni did not work full time. Harvard Business School reports that only 38% of its female MBA [master of business administration] graduates, during their childbearing years, work full-time.

Dr. Warren Farrell, author of the book, *Why Men Earn More*, found that a key reason men earn more than women is number-of-hours worked. In addition to providing abundant statistics, he interviewed a number of successful senior executive women. Each one stated that crucial to their success was their willingness to work longer than most women are [willing to]. For example:

When I interviewed Lillian Vernon, (of Lillian Vernon Corporation [a mail order company]), she said, "Many people who dream about their own businesses and don't have one, are not prepared to work that hard—to think about their job while they're getting dressed, showering, waiting for somebody—to think of every minute as an opportunity."

Theresa Metty, senior VP [vice president] at Motorola agreed, "Successful people don't see after-hour 'demands' as demands, but as opportunities. The opportunity to surprise, invent, create . . ."

All this doesn't surprise me. Having been career coach to 2,000 professional clients, 2/3 female, I know that more women than men prioritize work/life balance, wanting more time for family, home, friends, and recreation.

Women Want to Work Less

In the privacy of my office, many capable, highly educated women who, in public, may mouth politically correct mantras decrying the dearth of women in the boardroom, admit that what they'd really like is to work part-time if at all, and only on a pleasant job, so they can have ample time for home, family, friends, etc. Far fewer women than men are willing to work 58+ hours a week and to take work home or do extensive after-work professional development activities during evenings and weekends.

Steven Rhoads, author of the book *Taking Sex Differences Seriously* cites study after study indicating that the main reason most women want ample family time is their biological drive to have children and be the primary family caregiver. Feminist activists argue that is social conditioning by "the male hegemony." But if that were true, then why do women take on most family care giving in every society from Iceland to New Guinea, in every era from ancient times to today, and in all political contexts from communist to capitalist? Women's desire to prioritize family care giving is mainly biological predisposition, not cultural brainwashing.

Some women argue that it's men's fault that women don't spend more time at work. For example, *Career Journal* senior correspondent Peril Capell wrote, "If more women had men at home doing for them what women traditionally do for men, they might be able to stay at the office longer."

Fact is, many women don't do it for men. They do it for themselves. On average, it is women, more than men, who want to have children. So it is unfair of them to insist that the men share heavily in the child rearing.

Domestic Pleasures

It is the woman, on average, who cares more about having lots of time with children. (And the data don't support the importance of that—after controlling for socioeconomic status, quantity of time matters little. Quality of time does.) Even many wealthy women, who could afford and have access to high-quality child care, choose to forego that so they can be with their children. If quantity of family time matters more to women, it is unfair for them to impose that value on their husbands.

And regarding domestic chores, most men aren't as concerned about a tastefully decorated and sparkling clean home. On average, women care more about this.

It is unfair for women to force men to spend time on what the woman wants. If a man were to insist that a woman devote equal time to the things *he* cares about—for example, financial and tax issues, that fix-it/build-it project, or playing basketball, most people would think that unfair, selfish. Yet when women do it, we're expected to consider it reasonable.

I predict that if women—before they got married—informed their career-minded future husbands that they insist he fully share domestic and child-rearing responsibilities and that they don't expect to earn much money, many men would decide it isn't worth getting married. So, most women withhold those demands until afterwards.

Dreams Versus Ambition

A 2004 study by Catalyst, a women's advocacy organization, found that women aspire to senior executive positions at the same rate as men. But a woman (or a man) can't have it both ways. If she wants a moderate workweek, for the reasons I will outline below, she cannot fair-mindedly aspire to the boardroom.

Corporations, governments, and non-profits need plenty of good 20 to 40 hour-a-week workers, but not in the top spots. Here's why.

Imagine you were the CEO of a company and were considering two employees for a senior position. Candidate A had—over her or his 20-year career—worked 50 to 60 hours a week, and in spare time, made great efforts to keep upgrading skills. Meanwhile, Candidate B worked 40 hours a week, and in spare time, focused on family, home, friends, and recre-

Correlation between Hours Worked and Career Advancement

Average Hours Worked Per Week

	Men	Women
Lawyers	47.5	43.0
Management, business, and financial operations occupations	46.1	40.4
Doctors (primary care physicians)	50.0	45.0

Percentage of Workers in Top Jobs

	Men	Women
Lawyers (partner)	84.4%	15.6%
Corporate officers in the *Fortune* 500	84.3%	15.7%
Top-earning doctors	93.4%	6.6%

TAKEN FROM: Linda Tischler, "Where Are the Women?" *Fast Company*, February 2004.

ation, and had taken years off to raise children—thereby losing professional contacts and currency with the latest information and technology. You'd almost certainly hire Candidate A. Fact is, more men than women are like Candidate A. That, and not a sexist glass ceiling, is the main reason why women represent only 11% of senior executives in Fortune 500 companies.

But let's say that you, the CEO, did what feminist activists advocate: install a family-friendly workplace that prioritizes work-life balance, and hired many women who had worked only 40 hours a week and taken years off to raise children. You might hire lots of people like Candidate B. If so, your company would likely go out of business.

Here's why. Your competitors would hire lots of Candidate As. That would result not only in those senior executives—the company's more important people—being more productive, but their supervisees too. Dedicated, passionate leadership is infectious.

The Corporate Culture of Enthusiasm

A company with such committed employees is an exciting, passion-filled place. The argument that working more than 40 hours a week is ineffective and leads to burnout is not true. What leads to burnout is meaningless or too difficult work in a passionless workplace, not additional hours of meaningful, doable work in a passionate environment. Some of the most alive people I know work long hours. The argument that working more than 40 hours a week leads to burnout is unsupported by sound research. Such rhetoric is a shoot-from-the-hip pitch that feminist advocates use to sell work-life balance to employers. We all know how being around dedicated people makes us more energized, not less.

A workplace with long- hard-working passionate people results in the company's products being better or more cost-effective, which makes thousands of people—the customers—happier. Aren't you grateful when your home, TV, car, etc., is wonderful, reliable, and didn't cost too much? Creating excellent products, in turn, causes a company's profits to grow, which allows the company to invest in more innovation, provides money to the thousands of shareholders who entrusted their savings to the company, and increases the sense of pride and passion among the company's employees.

Meanwhile, your employees, mostly Candidate Bs, zealots for work-life balance, in the short-run, will appreciate being able to leave work earlier than workers at your competitors' companies. When, in the middle of a brainstorming meeting, someone says, "Sorry, I have a parent-teacher conference. I have to leave," and you say, "Fine," everyone will smile at how family-friendly their workplace is. But inside, those with passion about their work will feel that passion just slightly diminished. Each such event—for example, every time an employee takes advantage of the Family Leave Act—diminishes your workplace's passion just a little more. A number of your employees, who had taken years off to raise a family, are less up-to-date and lack current professional contacts. In the intermediate term, your employees will be working for a company in decline because their competitors, filled with more passionate, dedicated, more knowledgeable, better connected employees, are producing a better product. And in the long-term, such companies are far more likely to go out of business, leaving your boardroom with 0 percent women and 0 percent men.

Reexamining the Work-Life Balance

The media's headline message is, "Hire more women and make the workplace more family-friendly. Stop demanding that executives work 50 to 60 hours a week. Be more like France that mandates a 35-hour average workweek." The media is far less eager to trumpet the fact that despite France having a better educated population and 35-hour work week, its unemployment rate is more than twice the US rate and there's talk of changing the law. Advocating "family-friendly, work-life balance" workplaces will likely create different headlines a few years from now: "More jobs offshored to India." "More companies open new facilities in China." "Unemployment soars."

For the reasons stated at the outset, if I were a CEO, I would certainly want to hire women in senior positions, but only those with a proven track record of having put in long hours at work and in professional development, and who could be counted on to continue doing so. Those are the same criteria I would use to evaluate male candidates.

Women, if you want to be considered for the boardroom, it doesn't cut it to say you're working smart so you needn't work long hours. There are plenty of men competing for those slots who work both long and smart. You can't have it both ways: either plan on working long and smart or accept a lower-level job in exchange for work-life balance.

There would be plenty of room in my company for women and men who want to work a moderate workweek, but not at the top. I don't care whether my executives have a Y-chromosome, but I want their priority not to be work-life balance, but rather helping my company to ethically develop the best products in the world.

> "While both male and female styles of leadership can be effective, 'female' frequently has the edge."

Women Make Better Corporate Leaders

Joanna L. Krotz

Joanna L. Krotz writes about small-business marketing and management issues. She is the coauthor of the Microsoft Small Business Kit *and runs Muse2Muse Productions, a custom publisher located in New York City. In the following viewpoint, she maintains that men and women are equal in capability but have different leadership skills, and in today's business climate women's leadership qualities better lend themselves to success than men's do, she contends.*

As you read, consider the following questions:

1. According to the author, what are some strengths of the female leadership style?

2. How does a female leader's understanding of relationship dynamics influence employees, as described by Krotz?

Joanna L. Krotz, "Do Women Make Better Managers?" *Microsoft Small Business Center,* 2006. Courtesy of Microsoft Corporation.

3. If women are generally better leaders than men, why are they still underrepresented in positions of power, according to Krotz?

Before getting to the point of this provocative [title], here's a disclaimer: Prepare to consider widely accepted generalizations.

Translated, that means, "Included in this article are some sweeping statements presented as general truths but based on limited or incomplete evidence."

But let me add this: Remember, too, that being equal does not mean being the same. Now, let's proceed.

As women gain traction as business owners and executives, gender differences are increasingly playing out in the way they run their shows. If you think that isn't having an effect on the rules of the business road, think again.

Nearly 11 million privately held companies are now majority-owned (50% stake or greater) by women, according to the Center for Women Business Research, based in Washington, D.C. That accounts for nearly half (47.7%) of all private companies in the United States. In addition, women-owned companies now generate $2.5 trillion in annual sales and employ 19 million people nationwide.

Typically, women operate and manage those businesses in some significantly different ways than men do. Recent studies point out that while both male and female styles of leadership can be effective, "female" frequently has the edge.

Obviously, no single individual can embody every one of the many traits we tend to call "female" or "male." In exploring such issues, we must allow for the sweep of imperfect generalizations.

With that understood, here's how women manage and why they often do it better than the guys.

Women Are More Flexible

As we all know, gender differences stem from nurture and nature alike. It's not only socialization that shapes men and women. It's also biology.

In the past few decades, researchers have discovered physiological variations in the brains of men and women. For example, male brains are about 10% larger than female brains. But women have more nerve cells in certain areas. Women also tend to have a larger corpus callosum—the group of nerve fibers that connects left and right hemispheres. That makes women faster at transferring data between the computational, verbal left half and the intuitive, visual right half. Result: Women are more flexible and find it easier to multitask. Men are usually left-brain oriented. That often makes them better at solving abstract equations and problems.

As girls and boys grow up, of course, they're also molded by differing sets of social rules and expectations. Gender obviously colors behavior, perception, and just about everything else.

Women Show Certain Leadership Strengths

Typically, when comparing managers, the dialogue is framed as men's command-and-control style versus women's team-building or consensus approach.

"Women managers tend to have more of a desire to build than a desire to win," says Debra Burrell, a psychological social worker and regional training director of the Mars-Venus Institute in New York. "Women are more willing to explore compromise and to solicit other people's opinions." By contrast, men often think if they ask other people for advice, they'll be perceived as unsure or as a leader who doesn't have answers, according to Burrell.

Other female leadership strengths:

- Women tend to be better than men at empowering staff.

- Women encourage openness and are more accessible.

- Women leaders respond more quickly to calls for assistance.

- Women are more tolerant of differences, so they're more skilled at managing diversity.

- Women identify problems more quickly and more accurately.

- Women are better at defining job expectations and providing feedback.

On the other hand, men tend to be more confident and faster decision-makers compared to women. Male managers are also more adept at forming "navigational relationships," that is, temporary teams set up to achieve short-term goals, says management psychologist Ken Siegel, whose Los Angeles firm, the Impact Group, works with executives to develop leadership.

What About "Hard Skills" and Analysis?

Big deal, right? So women typically outperform men at communications and interpersonal skills, which is far from a news flash. You're probably thinking: Those are "soft skills," not the hard tools and analysis required to grow a business.

How do such "female" traits translate into better business management?

In today's workplace, when employees juggle multiple jobs, and technology enables even the smallest businesses to compete in global marketplaces, the ability to make staff feel charged up and valued is a definite competitive edge.

"Some companies succeed while others don't," says Jeffrey Christian, chairman of Christian & Timbers, a Cleveland-based executive search firm. "It's not about production, it's about talent. Whoever has the best team wins."

Women in Politics Get Things Done

In 1991, almost none of India's village councils were headed by women; the 1991 constitutional amendment passed to redress this imbalance mandated the election of women as *pradhans*, or council heads, in a third of villages that were chosen entirely at random. This means the villages reserved for female candidates were no different from other villages before the women-only elections....

Communities with women as pradhans had larger quantities of key public services overall. Nor was quality sacrificed for quantity—facilities in the women-led villages were of at least as high quality on average as in the communities with traditional male leadership.

Ray Fisman,
Slate, *November 27, 2007.*

Money is not the primary reason talented people stay on the job or jump. Rather, they stay predominantly because of relationships. "Women get that," says Christian, whose firm placed Carly Fiorina at Hewlett-Packard, among other high-level hires.

Generally, women delegate more readily and express appreciation more often. "Women ask questions, men tend to give answers," says Terri Levine, a career coach based in North Wales, Pa., who often advises entrepreneurs.

By communicating goals more readily and expressing appreciation more often, women tend to be better at making staffers feel recognized and rewarded. That translates into cost-effective staffing and recruiting.

Experience Broadens Skills

Lately, women are demonstrating higher levels of traditional "hard" or "male" skills as well. Some investigators suggest that many women workers had such skills all along, but that male bosses either overlooked or misperceived them. Others think the cumulative years of experience for women are broadening their skills.

One influential study, conducted in 1996 by management consultant Advanced Teamware (since merged with ConsultingTools), analyzed a database of 360-degree assessments for more than 6,000 managers. Such assessments include anonymous reviews from a manager's peers, supervisors and subordinates. The study looked at a range of managerial behavior, including problem solving, controlling, leading, communicating and more.

The results:

- ". . . Previous studies showed that women excelled in interpersonal skills (right brain), not in intellectual skills (left brain). Our study demonstrates that women are considered better performers in both right- and left-brain skill areas."

- "Women received higher evaluations than men in 28 of the 31 individual behaviors, representing 90% of items."

- "The most problematic factor for women is Managing Self . . . The worst rated of the 31 behaviors is 'Coping with one's own frustrations.'"

More Glass Ceilings Ahead

Obviously, there are still very few women running Fortune 500 companies and, in the corporate VP [vice president] ranks, there are roughly three men to every woman. So if women have the managerial edge, how come you don't see more of them in positions of power?

Here's my speculation: Men are used to running the show and, for the most part, don't reward "female" style management because they see it as weak. Women have had to prove, repeatedly, that their way of managing works. (Then, too, women have only begun to rise on corporate ladders. Give them time.)

For owners of small and midsized businesses, being able to keep staffers and stakeholders enthusiastic may be the key factor in building success. "You want to delegate outcomes, not tasks," says consultant Siegel. "You must have the ability to let go. Women can do that better than men because their self-esteem is multifaceted," he says. "Men's self-esteem is based on what they do, it's uni-dimensional."

The upshot for chief executives should be to move over to the "female" side of management, whether you're a thorough-going left-brainer or a woman trying to manage "male." Turns out, girls can do it better.

Periodical Bibliography

The following articles have been selected to supplement the diverse views presented in this chapter.

Sarah Baxter	"American Psycho," *Times (London)*, April 22, 2007.
Elisabeth Eaves	"Why Do Women Turn Their Backs on Science?" *Forbes*, March 6, 2009.
Peter Grant	"Dame Show: Peter Grant Meets the Men Who Love Dressing Up in Panto," *Liverpool (UK) Echo*, December 8, 2007.
Andy Hsi	"Self-Destruction and the New Gender Role Crisis," *University of Southern California Daily Trojan*, August 30, 2006.
Timothy A. Judge and Beth A. Livingston	"Is the Gap More than Gender? A Longitudinal Analysis of Gender, Gender Role Orientation, and Earnings," *Journal of Applied Psychology*, September 2008.
Andrew Koppelman	"Why Phyllis Schafly Is Right (but Wrong) About Pornography," *Harvard Journal of Law and Public Policy*, Winter 2008.
Kristina Peterson	"Making a Splash: The Country's First Male Synchronized Swimming Team Breaks One Barrier, but Others Remain," *San Francisco Bay Guardian News*, January 18, 2006.
Richard N. Pitt and Elizabeth Borland	"Bachelorhood and Men's Attitudes About Gender Roles," *Journal of Men's Studies*, Spring 2008.
Elianne Riska and Aurelija Novelskaite	"Gendered Careers in Post-Soviet Society: Views on Professional Qualifications in Surgery and Pediatrics," *Gender Issues*, December 2008.
Christopher Shiels and Mark Gabbay	"The Influence of GP [General Practice] and Gender Interaction on the Duration of Certified Sickness Absence," *Family Practice*, April 2006.

OPPOSING
VIEWPOINTS®
SERIES

CHAPTER 4

What Gender Roles Will Males and Females Play in the Future?

Chapter Preface

In October 2008, the British Broadcasting Corporation (BBC) reported on an infertile couple who hired a woman in India to carry their embryo and deliver their baby for a payment of about $10,000. As Western women delay childbirth and infertility rates rise, "fertility tourism" to India is booming, especially among Europeans living in countries that do not allow women to be paid explicitly for bearing another woman's child. Even citizens of countries that do allow surrogate pregnancies (such as the United States and the United Kingdom) are turning to Indian women because fees are lower and more potential surrogates are available.

Pregnancy is just the latest service to be outsourced to a foreign country. People want babies, and if modern medical advancements make it possible to pay other women to carry those babies, many motivated prospective parents will do so.

The practice is not without controversy, however. The ability to bear children remains the one biological function women have in distinction from men. With the appearance of reliable contraception in the twentieth century, women gained the power to control when they wanted to conceive and carry children. In the modern world, a single woman can procure sperm very easily and become pregnant without a male partner; a single man cannot become a parent just by procuring some eggs. But technology that enables artificial insemination and in-vitro fertilization—requirements for surrogate pregnancy—has now eliminated the need for men to partner with women if they want to become fathers. In addition to worrying about the exploitation of poor women and the treatment of babies as marketable goods, critics lament that the absolute separation of pregnancy from motherhood undermines a woman's role and reduces her value to the economic worth of her uterus.

Proponents argue that surrogate pregnancy has liberated men and women from the need to find reproductively compatible partners with whom to build families. They maintain that separating (personal) biology from parenthood gives people the opportunity to form relationships that were unimaginable in the past. In an increasingly intellectual, information-driven global society—in which women no longer need men around to do the heavy lifting and men no longer need women around to bear their heirs—people are able to interact as individuals with unique talents and interests and not just as representatives of separate, biologically derived, gender-constrained groups. For some, the historical reason to form male-female partnerships—procreation—has disappeared.

Reproductive technology, such as surrogate pregnancy, is just one means by which men and women are circumventing biological limitations; other modern technologies also reduce the distinctions between male and female gender roles by providing individuals of one sex equal access to opportunities formerly restricted to the opposite sex. The following chapter addresses the seeming convergence of gender roles and explores the trend against the reality of genetic history and biological, cultural, and gendered identities.

> "Straight men are liberating themselves
> from homophobia, leaving themselves
> open to gay influence, and thus to a
> more expansive idea of what it means
> to be a man."

Men Are Becoming More Like Women

Chris Nutter

Chris Nutter is a contributor to The Gay & Lesbian Review Worldwide *and is the author of* The Way Out: The Gay Man's Guide to Freedom No Matter If You're in Denial, Closeted, Half In, Half Out, Just Out or Been Around the Block. *The following viewpoint discusses the rise of metrosexuality in recent years and the impact it has on straight men's perceptions of gay influences. According to Nutter, TV shows like* Queer Eye for the Straight Guy *and* Will and Grace *have helped straight men embrace things previously labeled as "gay," and have helped decrease homophobia.*

As you read, consider the following questions:

1. What kind of man is seen as being "metrosexual," according to Nutter?

2. According to the author, where and when was the term "metrosexual" first used?

3. What are some ways that popular culture is redefining the ideal straight man, in Nutter's opinion?

In July 2003, Bravo premiered *Queer Eye for the Straight Guy*, a reality series in which five urbane gay men give lifestyle makeovers to straight men, and it became an overnight cultural phenomenon. That same summer, the *New York Times* made the coinage "metrosexual"—a straight guy who grooms himself like a stereotypical gay guy—a household word. Both of these pop culture phenomena reveal that a gay makeover of the straight American male has literally reached prime time. While the media's reporting on the subject revealed the obvious—that indeed straight men are looking more gay these days—the real and radical change in straight American men has gone virtually unnoticed. Much more than a matter of heterosexual men simply working out, waxing, and wearing Prada, straight men are liberating themselves from homophobia, leaving themselves open to gay influence, and thus to a more expansive idea of what it means to be a man.

Declining Homophobia

No longer averse to "gay traits" in the way that straight men of Ronald Reagan's and John Wayne's generation were, the new American man has made his way out of this narrow, homophobic ideal of manhood and embraced a larger world. Those in the vanguard include actor Eric McCormack of *Will & Grace*, who has said that Will is close to his own (non-gay) personality; San Francisco mayor Gavin Newsom, who has become a leading gay activist; and the Carlson twins modeling in unabashedly homoerotic poses for Abercrombie & Fitch. Right behind them is every straight guy who auditioned to go on prime time TV to be made over by a team of gay men.

Call him the "post-straight" American male. The rise of the post-straight male constitutes a drastic shift in the Zeitgeist [spirit of the times], because in traditional American culture homophobia in men has not only been indulged, it has been respected. And the impact of this phobia was by no means limited to maintaining the great divide between straight men and gay men. Anything associated with male homosexuality— from dancing and creativity to male beauty and friendships with women—has been stigmatized, too, estranging the straight American male from human traits erroneously labeled as "gay." Exerting what is surely the greatest impact on American manhood since the rise of feminism in the 1970's, gay liberation is not only helping to heal relationships between straight men and gay men, it is also allowing "gay" qualities back into the construction of masculinity, and many straight men are realizing that they've been on the losing end of homophobia, too.

Changing Expectations

This tectonic shift in the expectations of straight American men did not happen overnight but instead belongs to a movement that's been underway for decades. As gay liberation spread in the 1970's and 80's and gay men quietly and bravely came out to their straight friends and relatives and broke new ground for what was acceptable and even desirable in men, there emerged a more open, expressive, gay-friendly male character. Even when it was illegal for gay men to congregate in bars or clubs, and homosexuals were regularly thrown in jail, fired, kicked out of their homes, and given shock treatments as "cures," there were straight men who defied homophobia. Actually, gay men in big cities have known of the cool straight man's existence for decades. He was the heterosexual hair stylist at the salon in the Village, the straight DJ at the disco in the Castro, and the fag-hag's boyfriend in West Hollywood who embraced her gay friends.

Also appearing in gay-oriented books and films, this guy was the straight character who lived or worked in gay environs, or the straight actor who played gay roles with no loss of empathy for the character. For example, in the 1968 play and 1970 film *The Boys in the Band*, actor Cliff Gorman brought to life the character of Emory, the quintessential "nelly queen," and did so with a realism and complexity that made it hard to believe it was a heterosexual man in the role. In *Tales of the City*, which the *San Francisco Chronicle* began to serialize in 1976, Armistead Maupin created the character of Brian Hawkins, a straight man who lived, worked, and socialized in the gay universe of 1970's San Francisco.

In the 1970's and early 80's Broadway choreographer and director Bob Fosse was defying practically every limit on the straight male identity, first by succeeding in a world dominated by gay men, then by daring to be "flamboyant" in the choreography of his Broadway shows, notably *Cabaret*. World-famous party promoter Ian Schrager, the straight half of Studio 54, helped usher in the era of "gay cachet" by turning disco, hitherto a gay cultural phenom, into a national craze. Republican Senator Barry Goldwater, considered the father of modern conservatism, became an open advocate for gay rights when his grandson came out of the closet, years later taking a stand against the ban on gays serving in the military by writing in *The Washington Post* that "you don't have to be straight to shoot straight." Phil Donahue spoke publicly about his own journey out of the homophobia of his working-class Irish upbringing and became the first TV host to present gay men in a fair and open light.

Metrosexuality Gains Prominence

Still, with the homo-averse image of Ronald Reagan still representing the American male ideal, this alternate straight man remained ignored in the 1980's, or under suspicion for being gay himself. (Even Bob Fosse in his 1979 autobiographical

159

film *All That Jazz* included the death-bed epiphany that his compulsion to sleep with slews of women probably came from his own fear that deep-down he must be homosexual.) It was in the 90's that the post-straight male started to gain prominence. In 1992, presidential candidate Bill Clinton became the first candidate for national office to court the gay vote and to speak out against homophobia. Also in that year, Calvin Klein hired Herb Ritts to photograph a shaved, plucked, and pumped Mark Wahlberg in classically objectifying homoerotic poses for Calvin Klein underwear, and did the same with Antonio Sabato, Jr., four years later. In 1993, Tom Hanks portrayed a gay man in the movie *Philadelphia* and later thanked his gay mentor in his Oscar acceptance speech.

By the late 90's the examples in the media of this transformation became innumerable. *Will & Grace* debuted in 1998 and became one of the hottest shows in the country. Not only was the leading gay character played by a heterosexual man who classified himself in an interview with Diane Sawyer as "sexually straight, but socially gay"—a social creature theretofore known only to gay urbanites—the ratings for the show were so high that it was clear that many straight men were tuning in each week and getting a pretty massive infusion of gay culture (or at least a TV version thereof). This included prominent depictions of a reversed world of straight men in the gay mix—as with Woody Harrelson's role as Grace's boyfriend learning what it's like to be in the minority, seeing life through a gay cultural prism, learning the art of playing gay, and ultimately understanding Grace better through her relationship with Will.

A number of movies reinforced *Will & Grace*'s depiction of the famous attraction between gay men and straight women, notably *My Best Friend's Wedding*, *The Object of My Affection*, and *The Next Best Thing*, which was further reinforced by such famous real-life friendships as the one between Madonna and [gay actor] Rupert Everett. In addition, many of the most popular shows in the country—from *Six Feet Under* and *Sex and the City* to *South Park* and *Spin City*—had leading straight male characters who were very open to their gay counterparts and to their own "gay" qualities. And in the Oscar-winning movie *Gods and Monsters*, Sir Ian McKellen's older sophisticated gay character brought Brendan Fraser's young brute out of his homophobic cloister and into a new world of expression and connectedness, encapsulating in fiction a process clearly under way in the larger culture.

Redefining the Ideal Straight Man

Straight men also became inundated with gay-inflected images of themselves. Abercrombie & Fitch turned homoerotic into hetero-erotic with their Carlson twins campaign, objectifying two all-American straight boys in the same way that straight men have traditionally objectified women. (Of course, they were also pitching to the gay male audience through these images, further shifting the power dynamic between gay men and straight men by placing straight men in the role of conforming to gay men's ideals.) Even national "man's man" magazines like *Men's Journal*, once content with cover stories on fly fishing, began to put sexy, half-naked guys on the cover, creating a look that could easily be confused with soft-core gay porn, complete with teasers promising the reader gorgeous abs. Puff Daddy's signature fashion line "Sean John" turned what was once quintessentially "gay" into something "gangsta" by debuting a line of Liberace-inspired, full-length fox furs for men.

Since the turn of the millennium, there have been other revolutionary moments, such as the arrival of the Bravo reality dating show *Boy Meets Boy*. Heralded as the first dating show to feature gay men—and then trashed for being as vapid as its heterosexual counterparts—there was one spectacular element. In the mix of men vying to be chosen by the lead were a few straight men pretending to be gay. Many gay groups were up in arms about this, observing that straight dating shows don't sneak gay people in to trick the lead. (That would soon change.) But when the straight men gave post-show interviews, each revealed that he had experienced an epiphany about the illusory nature of the difference between straight and gay men, while gaining insight into what life is like for gay men in the closet.

But it was Bravo's *Queer Eye for the Straight Guy* that turned hundreds of years of deep-seated conventional wisdom about American men on its head. While only a make-over show, it resonated with the viewing public because it mirrored something that was happening in the larger culture: gay men were rewriting many of the rules that defined the ideal straight man. Perhaps it was inevitable that labels would soon pop up to describe this new type of male who, while not homosexual, seemed in some ways to be "gay." Terms like "stag-hag" (a play on "fag-hag") and "stray" (for "straight-gay") were applied to straight men who hung around gay ones. "Straight but not narrow" described straight men who weren't hung up about homosexuality. The coinage "hetero-gay" was soon replaced by "metrosexual" to describe straight men who cared about their looks as much as gay men reportedly do.

The Beginning of the Metrosexual

Actually, the term "metrosexual" was coined some ten years ago [in 1994], in England, and appeared in *Salon* about a year before *The New York Times* used it in 2003. However, it languished in obscurity until *Queer Eye* made the idea of gay influence on straight men undeniable, and thus the concept of the metrosexual acceptable. The fact that the metrosexual has become widely accepted is significant because it normalizes the idea of a "gay influence" on straight men, traditionally a taboo subject. But the metrosexual is in and of himself a very narrow character defined almost exclusively by his gay inflected appearance—specifically his worked-out, moisturized, hip urban look, which relatively few gay men even possess. As such, it is limited to the realm of style. But this notion is also quite subversive because it represents a straight adoption of the classically gay experience of being sexually aroused by one's own body. It also indicates that straight men have morphed into objects of beauty and not just of power, or have at least merged the two qualities. Way ahead of the curve in this regard was Arnold Schwarzenegger, who was quite the willing "girlie man" when he posed in the early 70's for gay magazines like *After Dark*.

If it was the common cause of women's liberation that brought straight women and lesbians together in the 1960's and 70's (though the relationship was at times contentious), it is gay liberation that has begun to close the divide between straight and gay men. Think of it as straight men's own gay liberation, just without the gay part. After all, it is much more than one's sexual orientation that's liberated when one comes out; it's also the fear of exhibiting supposedly "gay" traits, as one begins to un-learn the internalized constraints on self-expression. Many heterosexual men are having a similar experience freeing themselves from homophobia and allowing themselves to be exposed to a definition of manhood perpetuated by gay culture that includes traits not associated with traditional masculinity.

Some Complications

While the rise of the post-straight male clearly indicates a monumental change in the culture of heterosexual American men, there are of course nuances and countertrends that make the observation of this new identity somewhat more complicated.

First, the post-straight consciousness as defined here is mostly a white cultural phenomenon. Black and Latin cultures are on separate paths with respect to gay liberation, so the dynamics of homosexuality and gay influence are playing them-

Emerging Metrosexuality in Kenya

Dennis Okanga carries lip balm in his coat pocket and cannot leave the house without applying moisturising lotion on his face and body. He also has a manicure and pedicure every two months and parts with an exorbitant amount for an intensive facial.

The 34-year-old lawyer is a sharp dresser who follows fashion trends religiously. As a result, he spends a tidy sum on clothes, shoes and accessories. A single man, his house always looks immaculate, thanks to someone who comes once a week to do the cleaning. For him, image is everything.

"I wasn't always keen on grooming and cleanliness and only started paying attention to my appearance after graduating from university," he says, adding that his profession probably played a role in this change.

Does he consider himself a metrosexual man? This is the man that has been described as an urban male with a strong aesthetic sense who spends a great deal of time and money on his appearance and lifestyle. Another school of thought simply labels him a man with the vanity of a woman.

But Dennis is quick to insist that neither of the descriptions fit him. "I am simply a man who likes to dress and look good."

Caroline Njung'e, Daily Nation *(Kenya), January 10, 2009.*

selves out differently in each group. For instance, in black culture, the word "gay" is often associated with "white," and most black and Latin men who have sex with men do not identify as gay. Also, many of the straight male constraints that are liberated by the post-straight consciousness—such as the idea that "real men don't dance"—exist predominately in white culture. Although these racial and ethnic differences make the picture more complex, they do help to illuminate the illusions we hold so dear about what constitutes a gay trait or a straight one; to wit, you'll have a hard time convincing a straight black Brazilian man that swaying his hips when doing the samba makes one "gay."

The second complication relates to the widespread tendency to conflate gayness with femininity. Homophobia has many of its roots in a hatred of the feminine. As the late Quentin Crisp observed about his trials and tribulations as an out gay man in World War II London, he wasn't despised because he was gay but because he was effeminate. Many straight men in the 1970's and 80's made the genuine attempt to relate to and identify with their feminine side (Dustin Hoffman in *Tootsie* and Alan Alda in general), while straight men in the 90's and 00's have explored their "gay" side (a la Patrick Swayze in *To Wong Foo* and Eric McCormack in *Will & Grace*). Is there a difference between the "feminine" and the "gay"? Perhaps—not at least in the minds of straight men. Either way, such manifestations in mainstream media reflect a sincere attempt to explore the other side of the sex-and-gender divide rather than simply to mock any transgression of it, as in, say, the gag drag of *Some Like It Hot* or the Blaine and Antoine sketches on *In Living Color*.

The third complexity is the entrenched presence of homophobia in American society, which is still espoused by everyone from the President to the Pope. The embodiment of the stiff, homophobic, right-wing male can still be found in plenty in NASCAR race audiences and evangelical churches everywhere. But it would be wrong to conclude that because homophobia persists in some quarters that the trend I've identified is confined to large urban centers in the so-called "blue states." Over the past six years I have interviewed dozens of straight men all over the country, most of them under forty, and this research has revealed a whole framework of subtle but deep gay influence at work in the "red states" and in the suburbs. Straight men from South Carolina, Michigan, and Mississippi frequently cited the impact of an older gay uncle or other relative who demonstrated an alternate way of being a man to counter their father's model. Surprisingly enough, almost every straight man I talked to reported that he'd been called "faggot" at one time or another, giving him some experience-based empathy with gay men and demonstrating that homophobia is as much a force for male conformity as against homosexuality.

Personal Experience

My own experiences growing up in Alabama and Mississippi match this assessment. My fraternity brothers in college helped open me up to the world, teaching me how to be affectionate with other men, encouraging me to be myself, and in their own ways nudging me out of the closet. Along with my actual brother, they were the first people to run to my side when I came out. A wonderful example of this release of homophobic tension in the heartland could be seen in a recent episode of the *Da Ali G Show* when the flamboyantly gay host Bruno revealed to a bunch of straight teenage boys on spring break in northern Florida that they'd been performing tricks for a (phony) gay TV show, and the boys simply laughed. For all its complexities, the overall trajectory of mainstream male culture is clear. Modern gay-inflected, post-straight icons like pop star Lenny Kravitz with his pink boas and perfect abs. Gavin Newsom with his perception that gay people feel for each other what he feels for his wife, and the straight guys on *Queer Eye* letting themselves be made over by a group of gay style mavens are demonstrating to an emergent generation of boys and men that flamboyance, compassion and openness are not contradictory to manhood or masculinity, nor are they "gay" qualities after all.

> "The rapidly growing sexual emancipation of American women . . . is diminishing the fundamental feminine factor in their character and personality, and turning them into quasi-males."

Women Are Becoming More Like Men

Boyé Lafayette De Mente

Boyé Lafayette De Mente is a journalist and author who has been writing about international and cultural topics for several decades. He is a weekly columnist at the Thunderbird School of Global Management and writes his own personal blog, from which the following viewpoint is taken. In it, De Mente explores how the status of women, especially U.S. women, has evolved since the 1960s and 1970s, when women gradually claimed for themselves the freedom and independence men enjoy. He notes that the sexual revolution of the period, however, has undermined the female "mystique" and eliminated many of the characteristics that used to distinguish the sexes.

Boyé De Mente, "Why American Women Are Becoming More Like Men! Cultural Factors That Are Reversing the Male-Female Roles," BoyeDeMente.com, March 2007. © 2007 Boyé Lafayette De Mente. Reproduced by permission.

As you read, consider the following questions:

1. According to the author, how did the United States' participation in the two world wars affect the lives of women and children?

2. How is female sexuality being exploited today in the United States, according to De Mente?

3. As explained by De Mente, how has the loss of mystery surrounding the female persona since the 1960s changed the behaviors of men and women in modern times?

It is common knowledge (not accepted by everybody) that males and females have a number of genetic traits that make them think and behave differently.

While the strength of these genetic attributes varies in individuals—sometimes to such a degree that neither the male nor female concerned behaves within the range that is typical and expected of their gender—the two sexes are usually different enough that they have traditionally thought and lived in two different worlds.

From the beginning of human history there was both figuratively and literally a man's world and a woman's world, and in most societies these two worlds were separated by barriers that were natural as well as those that were created by men to control women.

This latter factor—the creation of artificial barriers by men to control women—apparently came about for the simple reason that human males, like their lower-order animals relatives, were driven by instinct to control the females in their group so they would have guaranteed sexual access to them.

At first this male rationale was no doubt an individual thing. But as time passed and spirits and gods were created, men made their dominance over women a spiritual thing mandated by their godly creations—so they could attribute their superiority to the divinities and not have to take any guff from females.

Of course, there have been a number of known societies that were ruled over by women but these women did not become rulers as a result of their own abilities or actions. They invariably inherited their exalted positions because they were members of a ruling family that failed to produce a male heir.

A Divine Afterthought

In short, the obvious animal origins of the human race resulted in females automatically being treated as inferior by larger, stronger males, and then when males got around to creating gods they made sure that their gods "created women" as an afterthought to serve men, sexually and otherwise.

This situation has existed virtually unchanged until recent times—and still today exists to varying degrees in a number of societies, with the largest and most obvious of these being Islamic and Christian. Both Christianity and Islam have traditionally based one of the rationales for their existence on keeping women in their place—meaning uneducated and subservient to men.

The first colonists who came to America had, of course, been programmed in the rigid, anti-feminine and inhumane sexual taboos that prevailed in England and elsewhere in Europe at that time. These religious-oriented concepts continued to make a travesty of the sexual lives of both men and women—but especially women—throughout the early history of the United States.

The same outmoded concepts of the proper role of women in all areas of life continued to prevail until the mid-1900s. It may seem unimaginable now but American men who had long regarded themselves as the most enlightened people on the planet, did not permit women to vote until well into the 20th century.

And still today there are many areas of life in the United States that are either totally forbidden to women, or they are discouraged from attempting to enter these areas. But this long practice of holding women down and denying them the chance to develop their potential, sexually and otherwise, is now having astounding and unanticipated consequences.

Beginning in the last half of the 19th century a few women began to poke tiny holes in the barriers that men had erected against the entire female race ... to keep them in their place. As the years passed, these holes gradually grew bigger and bigger as more and more women joined this earliest group of female pioneers who were determined to break down the male-made barriers that had penned them in and down since the dawn of human history.

The Influence of Two World Wars

Finally in the 1920s—after the upheaval of World War I had resulted in hundreds of thousands of women joining the workforce and doing jobs previously done only by men—the female revolution in the United States began in earnest.

Large numbers of women began to frequent speakeasy nightclubs, to drink and dance with what for the times was wild abandon. A short-lived but spectacular economic boom spurred the appearance of hundreds of thousands of cars that contributed to both more frequent and more intimate relations with men as well as helping to provide upper middle-class and upper class women with more independence than females had ever had before.

The advent of movies in the 1920s was soon to be a boon to the growing freedom of females in the United States—a technological advance that, like the automobile, was to have a fundamental influence on American society.

This female revolution was considerably muted by the depression of the 1930s but the entry of the United States into World War II in 1941 put it back on track—and it has been racing forward at full speed ever since.

Once again millions of American women entered the wartime workforce, and by the end of the war the economy of the country had grown so large with so many new "female-type" occupations that most of these millions never left the workforce when the war ended.

The war that took millions of young men away from home and resulted in so many women working out of the home changed the traditional family lifestyle and child-raising in fundamental ways. Women of all ages, including teenage girls, had a degree of personal freedom unprecedented in history—and once they had it there was no way they were going to let it go.

Girls and young women by the millions began to do the things that in the past only boys and men had done. Ordinary girls and women became more fashion conscious and more conscious of their personal appearance. They began to dress and to wear makeup designed to attract the attention of males. They became both more aggressive and more receptive in their relations with men.

The rapid increase in the number of motion pictures depicting the glamour and sex-filled lives of movie stars became a major influence on the attitudes and behavior of young females. The widespread proliferation of television from the mid-1950s added to the economic and social revolution that was remaking the mindset of American females.

Girls and women began to compete with males in school, in the workplace and in all forms of recreation. In this new environment, the idea that sexual passivity was the natural lot of females began to fade—something that many young men applauded but they had no inkling about where this fundamental change in male-female relations could lead.

Smashing Sexual Restraints

The 1960s saw the blooming of the Hippie movement—a kind of social protest created by the young who were outraged by the faults they saw in the prevailing culture. A big part of this movement was doing away with virtually all sexual re-

k.d. lang and Androgyny

Music and the business of music is so sexually driven. . . . It depends, I guess, on how you were perceived. When women make their image about youth and sexuality, and not about intellect, that's kind of a dead-end road. . . .

"I've always had an interesting relationship with my androgyny," she says. "It's kind of breadfruit—it looks poisonous but it's really good once you figure out how to get into it. I think the combination of my voice and my look was pre-ordained." It has often been remarked on, this contrast between one of the most sensual rich voices, one that can floor you with emotion, coming from a woman with a practical haircut and a wardrobe of shapeless suits.

Every day, she says, she gets mistaken for a man. "I like that," she says. "I didn't always; it bugged me sometimes, but I like going through the world kind of ambiguous. I definitely get less harassment, less attention."

Emine Saner,
Guardian *(Manchester, UK), July 16, 2008.*

straints—a movement that resulted in many young women being able to explore and exercise their sexuality in ways that had not been available to females before.

From that period, the female revolution in the United States, promoted by movies, television, magazines and feminist books, became an overwhelming force that could not be slowed down, much less stopped. However, most of the impetus and power that the revolution gained was not specifically related to the aspirations of feminists or the self-motivated expressions of female frustration.

Much of the power of the movement came from the built-in male lust for profits that fueled the American economy. In short, publishers of magazines and books and producers of movies and television shows discovered that sex sells—and the one area of human sexuality that had never been really talked about, much less economically exploited, was female sexuality. . . .

Today, probably as much as 90 percent of all advertising and marketing programs in the United States are based on exploiting the sexual appeal of women. Teenage girls and young women in various stages of nudity make up a big percentage of all television fare. Most male as well as female pop singers are backed up by teams of semi-nude girls and women who hump and pump and gyrate in simulated sex orgies.

Destruction of the Female Mystique

This so-called entertainment has destroyed most of the mystery, most of the mystique, of feminine sexuality—ripping it away like the proverbial fiction-novel bodice. The subtlety that is a major part of male-female romance has also been dramatically diminished.

All of the positive attributes that have traditionally distinguished women—their mystery, their subtlety, that indescribable essence of femininity that made them so special—not to mention their importance and prowess in nurturing—have been diminished . . . more by the actions of money-addicted men than by the legitimate aspirations of women themselves.

Women are now far more sexually exposed and exploited than men, thanks to the over-reaction that has resulted from religious-oriented attempts to conceal and control the sexuality of women. . . .

The sexual restraints and taboos that misguided religious leaders placed on women in the early history of civilization condemned them to suffer the punishment of the damned— and still today makes the world of many women a Hell on earth. The rapidly growing sexual emancipation of American women is both good and bad. The good part is obvious. The bad part is that it is diminishing the fundamental feminine factor in their character and personality, and turning them into quasi-males.

As I noted in an essay on the diminishing of the stud factor in American males, there are now female boxers, female wrestlers, female weight-lifters, female body-builders (some with muscles that are grotesque), females who play football on mostly male teams . . . and female soldiers who are actually called upon to fight and kill.

I also pointed out that the more masculine the behavior of women, the more nature compensates by making the behavior of men more feminine. And vice-versa: the more feminine the attitudes and behavior of men, the more masculine females become in their thinking and behavior.

So as incredible as it is, men themselves have set the stage for American women to become more masculine—a phenomenon that has already changed the dynamics of male-female relations in the U.S. and will go much further before it reaches some kind of equilibrium . . . which could be that women will be permanently on top.

"Many more men are willingly pitching in at home these days, especially in caring for children."

Gender Equity Is Increasing

Marilyn Gardner

Marilyn Gardner is a staff writer for The Christian Science Monitor, *a daily international newspaper. In the following viewpoint, she describes the all-too-common disconnect between husbands and wives regarding the quantity and quality of housework that each spouse should perform in the household. Although most husbands still do not do as many chores as their wives do, Gardner notes, the trend is moving toward equal participation of the sexes.*

As you read, consider the following questions:

1. According to the author, at what point in a marriage does the imbalance between husbands and wives performing housework often begin?

2. As described by Gardner, why do women tend to worry more about completing household tasks than men do?

3. What, according to Gardner, is probably the best way to teach children that husbands and wives are equally responsible for housework?

When the subject is housework, Anne Ballentine describes her husband, Jeff, as "awesome." He cleans the downstairs of their home in Whitefish Bay, Wis., while she takes care of the upstairs. He does more than half of the laundry and cooking, and almost all the grocery shopping.

"My friends joke that he should run a husband camp, and others are hoping for cloning," says Mrs. Ballentine, who works for a healthcare system in Milwaukee.

Those clones would probably be worth their weight in gold, given that dust bunnies under the bed, dishes in the sink, smudges on the woodwork, and laundry in the hamper, are still contentious issues for many couples. Someone must do these tasks, but who?

For 21st-century couples, the answer appears simple in theory. But "we both will" often becomes "she will" in practice. Yes, many more men are willingly pitching in at home these days, especially in caring for children. But the gap between the amount of housework fathers do and the amount mothers do has actually widened slightly, according to Rudy Seward, a sociologist at the University of North Texas in Denton. Mothers in 2003 reported doing almost three times more housework than fathers, averaging 17 hours a week. Fathers reported spending six hours, on average—down from eight hours a week in 1989.

American women are not the only ones dreaming of husband camps and cloning to help the men in their lives perfect the fine art of wielding dust mops and dish cloths. In Spain, where half the men say they do no housework, a new law requires men to share domestic tasks. Beginning [in the] summer [of 2005], men must sign an agreement as part of a mar-

Girls Closing Math Gap

Gender differences in mathematics performance and ability remain a concern as scientists seek to address the underrepresentation of women at the highest levels of mathematics, the physical sciences, and engineering. Stereotypes that girls and women lack mathematical ability persist and are widely held by parents and teachers.

Meta-analytic findings from 1990 indicated that gender differences in math performance in the general population were trivial. However, measurable differences existed for complex problem-solving beginning in the high school years, which might forecast the underrepresentation of women in science, technology, engineering, and mathematics (STEM) careers.

Since this study of data from the 1970s and 1980s, several crucial cultural shifts have occurred that merit a new analysis of gender and math performance. In previous decades, girls took fewer advanced math and science courses in high school than boys did, and girls' deficit in course taking was one of the major explanations for superior male performance on standardized tests in high school. By 2000, high school girls were taking calculus at the same rate as boys.... Today, women earn 48% of the undergraduate degrees in mathematics.

Janet Hyde et al., Science, July 25, 2008.

riage contract in civil ceremonies. If a husband refuses to do his share, he could face penalties in a divorce settlement if the marriage fails.

While some see the law as "ridiculous" and "unenforceable," others consider it a reminder that it takes both partners to keep a household running smoothly.

Different Standards and Expectations

That's the message Joshua Coleman is trying to spread in his provocatively titled book, *The Lazy Husband: How to Get Men to Do More Parenting and Housework.* Assuming that husbands won't read it, he is targeting it to wives. "Women will have to lead the charge on this because men won't," he says.

When men marry, many assume they'll work out an arrangement that is roughly equal, says Dr. Coleman, a psychologist specializing in relationships. But once couples have children, many experience "a subtle or overt shift toward a more traditional gender division of labor."

Despite the finger-wagging adjective "lazy" in his title, Coleman emphasizes that many men aren't lazy. "They work hard in their jobs. They come home and do things around the house. But from the wife's perspective, if the kids are in bed and she's still doing dinner dishes at 11 and he's watching TV, it's understandable that she would call it lazy."

But women also contribute to the problem, he adds. Men often find themselves exasperated by their wives' exacting standards. Explaining this gender difference to bewildered husbands, Coleman says, "She sees dirt where you see nothing, she sees chaos where you see order, she feels tormented by dishes in the sink while you just see dishes in the sink." But women are also held to higher domestic standards than men. "If a house is a mess, people still don't blame the man nearly as much as the woman."

What Husbands Think vs. Do

Some men complain that even though they're doing more around the house, it never seems to be enough to satisfy their wives. A little appreciation goes a long way, they say.

"Too tired" to help is one of the excuses Coleman hears frequently from men. Others include "I don't know how," "I earn more than you, so I shouldn't have to do anything when I get home," and "I contribute in other ways."

Mark Hughes, a radio talk show host in Swarthmore, Pa., is candid about his domestic shortcomings. "I admit it, I'm definitely not doing my share of the housework," he says. Because he travels part of the week, the couple employs a baby sitter four or five half days. That enables his wife to take care of household chores.

When men do pitch in equally, wives speak in superlatives. Karen Wright of Mankato, Minn., calls herself "probably the most fortunate woman in America." Her husband, Jeff Pribyl, a chemistry professor, does "more than his share" of housework and child care and never complains, she says. He takes care of the laundry. Both vacuum, dust, and pick up the house. If one is busy, the other takes over.

Seeing this behavior as a child can often make a difference. Ms. Wright, operations director at a public radio station, notes that she and her husband both grew up with fathers who were fully involved in helping with domestic chores. "I think it's a natural for us," she says.

James Williams of Austin, Texas, also learned household skills from his father when he was growing up. Now married with two young children, Mr. Williams cooks, does dishes and laundry, mows the grass, and cleans the cat box, says his wife, Lauren. Both work full time.

Linda Kavelin Popov and her husband, Don, motivational speakers in Salt Spring Island, British Columbia, share the housework. Whatever task he's doing, she avoids criticizing. Her sanguine philosophy: "If he's going to do it, let him do it his way."

As more couples follow that advice and find their own way to divvy up inescapable chores, Coleman expects a domestic revolution to take place—someday. "It's getting better, it's changing, but there's still a long way to go," he says. "Everybody has to invent it for themselves."

> *"In light of alternative futures which exaggerate gender differences, the influence of gender on socialization will be great."*

The Future of Gender Roles Is Uncertain

Alexandra Montgomery

Alexandra Montgomery is a futurist researcher who studies trends and developments with families and children as society evolves in the twenty-first century. In the following viewpoint, she summarizes a workshop about how future economic and cultural trends could influence the structure of the family and the relative power and freedom of men and women within each of four scenarios: "Mr. & Mrs. Right Now," "Marriage Marketplace," "The Waltons for the 21st Century," and "Desperate Housewives."

As you read, consider the following questions:

1. According to Montgomery, which of the four proposed family scenarios is the least extreme?

Alexandra Montgomery, "US Families 2025: In Search of Future Families," *Futures*, vol. 40, May 2008, pp. 377–87.

2. As described by the author, what are some potential pitfalls of the "Marriage Marketplace" scenario?

3. What characteristics of the "Waltons" and the "Desperate Housewives" scenarios make them susceptible to severe separation of gender roles, as described by the author?

Looking back at the history of US families, sociologist Judith Stacey identifies a deep-seated slant in the US social sciences holding the "conviction that US family history would prove to be a global model," for family structure. With the onset of the industrial era, and US dominance in it, "Westerners presumed that the global diffusion of the modern nuclear family system would come about automatically." Instead, industrialization quickly gave way to a globalized information economy and the transition influenced families, both in the US and globally, to drift toward the "postmodern" state of "diversity, flux and instability." The meltdown of nuclear US families, Stacey notes, has contributed to a climate in which issues of gender, sexuality, reproduction, and family "are the most polarized, militant and socially divisive in the world." The intersection of topics such as these—gender, sexuality, and reproduction—in the US is known as the Culture Wars.

Driving Forces

By 1991 author James Davison Hunter had observed several issues (including abortion, separation of church and state, privacy, and homosexuality) representing polarities in US public opinion. What some have called backlash, Hunter's book *Culture Wars: The Struggle to Define America* explains as "a dramatic realignment and polarization that had transformed American politics and culture." The Culture Wars climate is one in which US society might be seen as "two warring groups, primarily defined not by nominal religion, ethnicity, social class or even political affiliation, but rather by ideological world views." Hunter's terms for these opposing worldviews are "Progressivism" and "Orthodoxy." Given the volatility of matters such as sexuality and reproductive rights to the domain of family, the Culture Wars stand out as an appropriate backdrop to future scenarios designed to explore the ways in which men and women might organize kinship, raise children, and define future gender roles. Its impacts cut across class lines, generating future outcomes that somewhat minimize dramatic socio-economic inequalities in the US but nevertheless highlight opportunities to address women's status.

While elected officials exploit "Family Values" as political currency, the idea of the "Long Boom" is an idea well-championed in Futures Studies literature. Futurist Peter Schwartz stated in 1997 that,

> We are watching the beginnings of a global economic boom on a scale never experienced before. We have entered a period of sustained growth that could eventually double the world's economy every dozen years and bring increasing prosperity for—quite literally—billions of people on the planet. We are riding the early waves of a 25-year run of a greatly expanding economy that will do much to solve seemingly intractable problems like poverty and to ease tensions throughout the world.

This sense of general optimism and security is countered by the other extreme: prolonged economic scarcity. The spectrum of possibilities between clashing moral matters and radical financial realities provides the opportunity to generate specific implications for the future of gender. The Long Boom vs. Scarcity and uncertainty also plays into the very essence of what has defined the US model of family since more than 100 years ago, "when industrialization turned men into breadwinners and women into homemakers by separating paid work from households." . . .

The uncertainties and trends were combined in different variations resulting in an end product from the US Families 2025 workshop consisting of four alternative futures, outlined in a scenario matrix where the vertical axis represents the status of the Culture Wars (Orthodox vs. Progressive) and the horizontal axis represents economic climate (Scarcity vs. Long Boom).

Description of Scenarios

Three of the resulting four future scenarios exemplify harsh extremes: Mr. & Mrs. Right Now. The New Waltons for the 21st Century, and Desperate Housewives offer little hope of female empowerment. Marriage Marketplace may be seen as a baseline future where business as usual means that future families will be run with entrepreneurial instincts and capitalistic goals, echoing its patriarchal underpinnings. The alternative futures are briefly described, then analyzed from the futures perspective with special emphasis on gender.

#1 Mr. & Mrs. Right Now

Transient relationships and equal economic partnerships characterize Mr. and Mrs. Right Now, which appears in the upper left corner of the matrix. Dire economic tensions and a social tide oriented toward progressive values produce families who forge non-kin emotional bonds by sharing of material resources. In this future, child rearing and living arrangements are somewhat communal because of the high cost of living and high unemployment. The emergence of a network of adults outside, who have concern for and influence over children, can be traced directly to the networks of adults sharing material resources for their own and their children's survival. Household arrangements and financial decisions are arrived at by consensus and necessity, and tend to be driven by what parents and pseudo-parents alike view as children's best interests.

#2 Marriage Marketplace

The Marriage Marketplace scenario occurs in the upper right corner of the matrix where there is strong economic growth and a stalwart sense of progressive values. The Marriage Marketplace is a fertile climate for a consumer paradigm of matchmaking. Unions are arranged and formalized through contracts, resumes, training, and certifications. Families blossom in a variety of legal forms (same sex, group, non-sexual, and/or no parent). There is an exponential increase in complexity of parenting and guardianship of children. There is little or no political, legal, or social pressure to conform to an ideal of marriage in the Marriage Marketplace. The idea is to find the best investment for one's personal social capital. Most notably, childrearing has become a thing apart from formal male-female relationships.

#3 The New Waltons for the 21st Century

The New Waltons for the 21st Century appear in the lower left corner of the matrix, representing the intersection of financial scarcity and a return to orthodox values. By 2025 the dual-income family has become nearly extinct and it becomes valued for women and girls to spend most of their time at work in the home, upholding family traditions, a fate which keeps many young women from completing high school studies. Extreme pockets of conservatism encourage arranged marriage and polygamy, partly as a means to solidify social networks and supplement a weak economy. Extended families living together combined with rising costs of caring for an average family's dependents (a combination of aging Baby Boomer parents and children) contributes to the fact that most families are barely scraping by. The burden of caring for aging parents and an overriding sense of emotional needs as a low priority create a highly survival-focused family climate.

#4 Desperate Housewives

Desperate Housewives appears in the lower right corner of the matrix, where traditional values prevail amidst advanced economic options for families in particular. The repeal of legislation making it possible for women to seek divorce creates an environment in which most marriages are largely kept intact. Economic security is guaranteed by men's role as bread winners, while women (some of them highly trained and educated) are pressured to marry and stay at home. Large families are affordable, thanks to financial incentives, and become something of a modern status symbol. Given the sharp decline of reproductive rights, US families are growing at a quicker rate than ever expected, and these realities in part determine the fate of women's lives. . . .

Baseline and "Worst Case" Scenarios

However dismal, the Marriage Marketplace scenario presents a future some may regard as the baseline, or most probable, future. Global capitalism flourishes, but family matters reveal the dark side of free markets where many, in this case low-income uneducated women, lose out. Since potential partners are evaluated by commercial standards, those who do not measure up to market whims will be dealt a poor hand. The same entrepreneurial values that create competition in the free market of husbands and wives might create a class of bankrupt social exchanges perhaps resembling legalized slavery or prostitution.

Furthermore, in Marriage Marketplace women and men become commoditized, and survival may depend on one's individual eagerness to fit the different molds, models, and stages of marriage, and the dehumanizing effect may be severe. In a consumer-driven market, mates are matched based on how well a potential partner satisfies a list of criteria. The openness of the marketplace, in theory, allows alternative and traditional domestic roles to flourish, but there will be a danger of exploitation. The free market yields to demands, especially from the persistent patriarchal worldview urging men to seek a female spouse/care giver to fill a so-called "traditional" mother role for future children. Will US women respond to this market? If not, who will? Immigrants? Clones?

Men, too, may suffer under a competitive system based on capitalist principles. Masculinity and femininity may both be exaggerated to obtain bids in the marketplace, and even same-sex relationships could demand extremes of male and female ideals which do little to advance equality. Progressive values will allow non-traditional or even radical arrangements to emerge, but how sustainable is the idea of using the law of supply and demand to determine what takes place in the family sphere?

The New Waltons represents a largely "Worst Case scenario" for families. Women are relegated to second-class status, but so is anyone else who may observe anything but traditional relationships—including step-families, same-sex partners, and the unmarried. The potential for abusive relationships is high, as many will remain entrapped out of financial necessity. Prejudice and discrimination are commonplace in regard to gender roles and sexuality.

In the New Waltons, future care of offspring and aging parents falls to females, while male counterparts enjoy the benefits of shifting all domestic labor and care giving to women. Women who can find work outside the home will take advantage of it, but it does not ease the burden of housework and care giving. Men, even those who are out of work, have little sense of duty to wives and/or the mothers of their children, and social problems that might ensue will invariably scapegoat women to justify the patriarchal system underlying extreme orthodox views.

Implications for Parenting and Children

In Mr. & Mrs. Right Now families become the focus of people's lives as an unexpected outcome of toned-down materialism, and the communal aspect of family allows for more adults than just biological parents to influence the lives of children. Men and women have more of an opportunity to equally partake in care giving, and not just families benefit from this shift; men may feel empowered by nurturing roles. On the other hand, Desperate Housewives is sure to eliminate close

U.S. Families 2025 Matrix

Mr. & Mrs. Right Now

Transient relationships

Economic partnerships

Child rearing somewhat communal

Marriage Marketplace

A cornucopia of trial & error arrangements

Entrepreneurial models of family and marriage

Sense of security provided by economic prosperity

The New Waltons for the 21st Century

Oppressed progressive enclaves

Extended families living together

Caring for aging baby boomers

Arranged marriages and polygamy

Desperate Housewives

Cohabitation socially prohibited

Denial of divorce

Financial incentives for keeping with tradition

Reproductive rights repealed

Alexandra Montgomery, Futures, *May 2008.*

extended family ties as the nuclear family ideal of contained self-sufficiency eliminates the need for wider social bonds.

In the Marriage Marketplace, parenting may become closely intertwined with science, as selectivity of offspring is as strategic as mate selection: designer babies will be common. There is the chance that some people will be subjected to biological breeding in order to meet market demands for sexual, reproductive, or genetic capital. Children will possibly be valued on the amount of time and financial investment they represent.

Implications for Roles and Equality

Children and adults in the Waltons and Desperate Housewives scenarios will be subject to increased gender-specific treatment, as the view of male and female becomes demarcated by strictly evolving roles: men as breadwinners, women as care givers. The emergence of arranged marriage and polygamy emphasizes women's low status. More so than the other scenarios, these particular futures will rely on female oppression. Repressing thoughts and emotions will be a way of life for the people, both male and female, living in this future. The norm will be to raise daughters to not question male authority, and social pressure may force hyper-masculinity on boys. The future potential of both genders could go underdeveloped because of strictly observed gender roles such as these. Offspring are important extensions of parents' ego and image, and in light of alternative futures which exaggerate gender differences, the influence of gender on socialization will be great. Fathers in the Desperate Housewives scenario have the most to gain from propagating large broods (financial incentives, increased social status), yet society would hold little expectation that men spend time in family life. Participating in the robust workforce defines men's purpose, marginalizing the growing numbers of fathers who seek a place as a nurturer. Men who do not marry or do not conceive many children may be stigmatized, or looked down upon, alongside the women who remain independent.

The Marriage Marketplace shows an increased partnership between men and women on a pragmatic basis, where day-to-day life involves adults working together in a seemingly egalitarian bargaining environment. As in the New Waltons for the 21st Century scenario, future economic scarcity serves as an impetus for female repression. In Desperate Housewives, women are literally trapped in compulsory marriages despite a sense of complacency brought on by economic abundance. There is the even larger matter of access to contraception that seals women's fate as mothers. Certainly a society that would repeal reproductive rights would have harsh penalties for adultery committed by Desperate Housewives.

The future of families examines the future of parenting and marriage, which can be expected to then define the normal roles of men and women in society. Globalization is changing the economic climate, with big impacts in store for the US, which may influence the ways we organize households, raise children, and observe social bonds. Globalization and the Culture Wars represent great uncertainties with concrete social and political implications for marriage and reproduction in the US. Documented trends and emerging issues, such as the stay-at-home-father movement, exploding immigrant populations, and changing attitudes toward material gain among young adults, further obscure the emergence of any one particular future for US families.

| "We are becoming more manipulative of
| our identity."

Gender Will Become a Choice

Karen Moloney

Karen Moloney is a chartered psychologist, consultant, writer, and speaker and a director of Moloney Minds in London. Her work includes advising companies on attracting and retaining top talent and building emotional capital within organizations—the creation of career and personal development opportunities to retain individuals. She is a fellow of the Royal Society of Arts and the Chartered Institute of Personnel and Development. The following viewpoint was presented as a lecture at the World Future Society Conference in 2007. In it, Moloney enumerates the biological differences between men and women and describes the ways humans are already able to tamper with gender.

As you read, consider the following questions:

1. According to Moloney, what traditional male roles are being undermined by advancements in science and culture?

2. In what way, according to the author, are prospective parents already controlling the outcome of a pregnancy?

Karen Moloney, "What Use Are Men? The Future of Sex and Gender," MoloneyMinds .com, July 8, 2007. Reproduced by permission.

3. By what means do people adopt some of the characteristics of the other gender, according to Moloney?

The brains of men and women are being investigated in ways previously not possible using CAT [computerized axial tomography] and functional MRI [magnetic resonance imaging] scanning. In summary, the main neurological differences both anatomically and functionally are:

Men's brains are bigger, women's are more densely packed and rarely switch off, the corpus callosum which connects the two hemispheres is denser and thicker in the female brain, men's brains tend to specialise, one area working at a time, women may use several parts of the brain at once, including sites on both hemispheres, to complete the same mental task.

The increased understanding of the effect of hormones, particularly testosterone, estrogen and progesterone cannot be underestimated. Some researchers are calling for revision of medical research techniques for drug trialling and dosage recommendations, lawyers are calling for high levels of testosterone to be taken into account in judging criminal activity in the same way that women's subjectivity to monthly hormone cycle has been used to mitigate charges of serious crime.

All of these physical characteristics, so obvious between us, anatomical, neurological, endocrinological impact upon our behaviour. It is no wonder, then, we often feel as if we're from different planets. . . .

The Erosion of Men's Traditional Roles

Procreator: For some time now, scientists have been busy divorcing sex from reproduction. In being able to freeze sperm, we no longer need lots of men around to impregnate women. Apart from the problem of biodiversity and the fact that all people would end up looking like just a few sperm-donor fathers, it would be possible to use the sperm we have lying in banks to produce several generations. This possibility has taken away one of the traditional roles of men, to provide one half of the necessary means of reproduction. With in-vitro fertilization, embryo selection and cloning, scientists have increasingly hijacked reproduction and made it possible outside of nature.

Father: Add to this the increase in the number of single women and lesbian couples choosing to raise families without a man present, and their role as fathers also diminishes.

Provider: Given the increased earning power of women and their ability to work and raise children at the same time, men's role as providers of the ever-needed financial support to dependent women is, if not redundant, then certainly reduced.

Protector: Their physical strength, which for millennia has been essential for survival, is now less of an issue. Modern warfare is more likely to require a degree in electronic engineering than an ability to throw a spear, and women, children and elderly, certainly in peaceful societies as we live in, don't need a male protector in the family, village, tribe like they used to.

Finally, the Y chromosome, which determines maleness, was ever fragile, and is becoming smaller and less important, leading to some scientists predicting it will disappear completely over forthcoming generations.

(In terms of women's traditional roles, we are losing out to scientific advances too. The first baby to be born in an artificial womb is within sight, eggs can be collected for in-vitro fertilizations and the same medical advances which apply to men will soon be felt in women.

Caring, which has traditionally been a female role, is being taken over by paid professionals as more women choose to work. So too is domestic work. However, unlike men, women are choosing to engage less in these roles and their diminution is not being forced upon them.) . . .

Men's Traditional Roles

By men being fierce, for example, angry, righteous, aggressive on behalf of women, children, the weak, elderly, those being bullied, men will continue to play an important protective role which women do not. Furthermore, men seem better able to divorce themselves from the feelings of those they oppose. In a conflict, men will defend more fiercely as they can be blinded to the other side's case. "They seem to operate", as one woman put it, "with less sense of guilt, they don't agonize, they are more action oriented than us."

Let's be clear. Women are also protectors; they protect institutions such as the family, the marriage, generations, entities, by building and maintaining relationships. They have been described as perhaps the glue that binds society together, but their protection is more long term than acute and different from the protection offered by a male.

Some women, particularly in countries where fewer women work still need men's financial support in order for them to raise the family.

Some men will enjoy increased responsibility for caring for the family and it will become more accepted in society for them to play this role. . . .

The erosions of traditional male and female roles that I have described are current, but from a futurist's perspective, I'm interested in whether they are a temporary glitch, or the signal of an emerging trend leading to a real shift in society.

Current Gender Role Shapers

- Societal beliefs about male and female roles

- Religion

- Position and power of women

- Balance of men and women in population

- Technologies enabling us to change gender

- Increased appreciation of differences and impact on our thoughts, feelings and behavior

- Increased independence of women

- Trend to women usurping men's roles

- Ability to determine the sex of our children

- Gender playfulness

Unpredictable Sources of Change

- Catastrophic genetic mutation

- Unforeseen contaminants affecting birth rates and sex of children born (for example the estrogen found in some foods is thought to be responsible for lowered sperm count and fertility in Europe)

- Government-imposed population and gender control.

However, something else is happening which is indicative of changes in society. We are wishing to be in control more and we are becoming more manipulative of our identity. Let me explain.

Controlling the Sex of Our Children

Most of us would find the idea of murder hateful, but in some countries, particularly those where the wrong gender would create considerable economic difficulties for the families, infanticide happens. In addition, science is allowing us now to find out the sex of our children before the age at which it is considered murder to abort a fetus. Considerably more people are choosing to terminate their pregnancies at this time and so determine the number of boys and girls they bear to term.

The effect this is having is to skew the distribution of the sexes across the world. In most societies where people wish to

The Gender Management Services Clinic in Boston

Dr. Norman Spack has treated young-adult transsexuals since the 1980s, and until recently he could never get past one problem: "They are never going to fail to draw attention to themselves." Over the years, he'd seen patients rejected by families, friends, and employers after a sex-change operation. Four years ago, he heard about the innovative use of hormone blockers on transgender youths in the Netherlands; to him, the drugs seemed like the missing piece of the puzzle. . . .

When Beth was 11, she told her mother, Susanna, that she'd "rather be dead" than go to school anymore as a girl. (The names of all the children and parents used as case studies in this story are pseudonyms.) For a long time, she had refused to shower except in a bathing suit, and had skipped out of health class every Thursday, when the standard puberty videos were shown. In March 2006, when Beth, now Matt, was 12, they went to see Spack. He told Matt that if he went down this road, he would never biologically have children.

"I'll adopt!" Matt said.

"What is most important to him is that he's comfortable in who he is," says Susanna. They left with a prescription—a "godsend," she calls it.

Hanna Rosin, Atlantic, *November 2008.*

choose the sex of their children, they are choosing to have boys. 70% of aborted fetuses in India are female. In China, the gender imbalance has reached serious proportions with 120 males born for every 100 females, (compare this to natural 105 to 100) representing a missing 20–40 million women.

The shortfall is being made up partially in trafficking, the police having released 42,000 kidnapped women over 2 years—2001–2003. As cheap ultrasound techniques become available at village level, we can expect this imbalance to continue. Several government initiatives such as Girl Care in China are underway to improve the respect and value of girls and in Fujian province, $24 million has been made available to enable girls to go to school for free.

Their rarity will increase their value anyway.

Although a process of negative feedback seems to increase the number of boy babies born during and after wars and in harems, suggesting nature has a way of replenishing her proportions, scientists have yet to understand why it hasn't begun working in contemporary China. Could it be that some men will start behaving as women when there is an imbalance in the population?

Controlling Gender

Most social scientists distinguish between sex and gender; gender being an individual's self-concept of being male or female, as opposed to their biological sex, the one they were born with.

Another method is opening up to scientists as they increase their understanding of not just what makes an embryo genetically male or female but what makes a male or female embryo think in ways that are masculine or feminine. When conception occurs, the mechanism by which the fused egg and sperm will become a boy or girl is much better understood. All embryos start life as female, remember, with internal female organs, but from six weeks if the baby is to be a boy the genes on the Y chromosome cause the fetus to develop testicles which then produce the male hormone testosterone. It's this testosterone that makes the male organs grow. If, however, something goes wrong with the delicate balance of hormones in the womb the child's genitals won't develop fully and can be ambiguous. As we increasingly understand the role of hormones and endocrine disrupters, such as phlalates, we may be inclined to manipulate both sex and gender.

Corrective hormone therapy or genetic patching could be given at adolescence to help increase or reduce the maleness and femaleness of the emerging young adult.

Using Hormones Recreationally

In adulthood, we have the chance to alter aspects of both sex and gender. For some time we have been able to treat genuine transsexuals with hormones and surgery. But it could be that the same hormonal treatments can be used for recreational purposes as men and women may be more willing to try out what it is like in the other gender. We already know that men are using testosterone to boost their sporting and sexual performance, but will women shortly be using it to boost their competitiveness at work, for example, or their sex drive post menopause?

If we can sort out the undesirable side effects and think like the other sex without coming to look like them, there could be future for this leisure pursuit. Recreational hormones may become freely available on the market, but probably safer would be the temporary stimulation of the part of the brain or endocrine system which releases the body's own hormone. For example, to be able to put on a helmet rather than take a cocktail of drugs so to stimulate the production of dopamine and create the feeling of being hopelessly in love, perhaps to relive an ended relationship. We might do this in the privacy of our own homes. . . .

Which Gender? You Decide!

In making personal decisions, you will have choices not just in how many children you have, but which sex, what physical characteristics, personality or talents they have. Despite all the risks of descending into a world of eugenics, designer babies already exist. Who you choose to have a relationship with and how to find a permanent mate will be decisions enhanced by increased knowledge about that individual and the possibility of changing him or her once you've chosen them. (OK, we'll buy this house but we'll put in an extra bathroom). And enjoying mind-enhancing experiences, not just those related to sex and gender, may become commonplace and so again, a choice you find you need to make.

In corporate life, knowing what you will know about for example the effects of testosterone on competitive behavior, who do you hire, fire, move, and how do you keep people performing at the highest levels at work as in sport?

Underpinning all of this is the more fundamental choice: are you ready to mess with nature?

"A post-gendered condition does not necessarily imply the end of all gendered characteristics; it merely signifies the end of fixed and traditional gender assignments."

Gender Will Become Obsolete

George Dvorsky

George Dvorsky is the cofounder and president of the Toronto Transhumanist Association and the publisher of the Sentient Development blog and podcast, where the following viewpoint originated. He is a leading proponent of transhumanism, a scientific, social, and philosophical movement that addresses the way future technology will allow people to transcend the limitations of their human bodies. In the following viewpoint, Dvorsky argues that if individuals no longer enjoy the benefits and endure the risks of fixed gender, then gender differences—and the politics and control that accompany them—will no longer interfere with what a person chooses to do in life.

As you read, consider the following questions:

1. According to Dvorsky, how has being born male placed a person at greater risk than being born female?

George Dvorsky, "Overcoming Gender," *Sentient Developments*, January 6, 2008. Reproduced by permission.

2. How would cybernetics be the ultimate liberator of women, as stated by Dvorsky?

3. What does Dvorsky say is the main goal of the transhumanist postgenderism movement?

Your gender is a constraint. This is an inalienable truism, regardless of whether you're a man or a woman.

We can no longer deny that males and females are profoundly different. The hallucination is over. Scientists and behaviorists are discovering that men and women differ not just physically, but cognitively and emotionally as well. These differences are not merely the result of gender-specific socialization; they are innate—the result of thousands of years of sexual competition and selection.

Your gender assignment and sense of sexual identity is an imposition. Like many of your other characteristics, you are largely the result of a genetic lottery that happened beyond your control. Consequently, you are in no small way predetermined. Your physical and psychological capabilities are very much constrained and dictated by your genetic constitution.

Sure, the environments that we find ourselves in and the ways in which we are socialized play a contributing factor to our health, personalities and broader perspectives. But let's not fool ourselves; each and every one of us has characteristics that are forever limited by our genetic code.

Barring the application of enhancement biotechnologies, I will never be able to conceptualize music as profoundly as Beethoven, nor will I ever be able to visualize numbers like Pierre de Fermat [a French mathematician]. No amount of studying, hard work or dedication will ever change this. *I am physiologically incapable of acquiring these capacities.*

Similarly, my gender plays an integral role in determining who I am, what my preferences are, and ultimately what I'm capable of.

And that bothers me.

Gender Is a Disease

Like the work being done to bring about a radical life extension revolution, and whose proponents argue that aging is a disease, we likewise need to change our perceptions about gender. There are a number of areas where we can see how our genders work to our disadvantage and why we would want to do something about it.

Men have the double-edged sword of being, in general, physically advantaged. While this tends to contribute to male dominance over women, it has also placed men in dangerous situations and environments. Males are conventionally the members of society who are sent into combat and are expected to perform hazardous—and sometimes sacrificial—work.

Aside from the overtly obvious physical dimorphism that separates men from women, there are also a number of cognitive and behavioral differences that work to stratify humans along gender lines.

Threats, physical assaults and homicides are an indelible male feature across all cultures and typically the result of male-male competition over resources that work to increase reproductive fitness. Males tend to have more accidents than females across their entire life spans. For every girl that is injured on a playground, four boys are likewise injured. Boys burn themselves more than girls. Roughly twice as many females across all ages suffer from significant levels of anxiety and depression than their male counterparts; women are more prone to suffer from eating disorders and post-traumatic stress disorder.

Looking at latent cognitive abilities, boys and men have slightly higher average IQ scores than girls and women. Females across all ages consistently outperform boys and men on tests that assess the speed of matching arbitrary symbols to numbers. In measures of sensitivity to verbal cues, females almost always outperform males.

Needless to say, these gender differences are general tendencies. Men and women do not all fall within these parameters. But what these statistics reveal is that across the entire population males and females are stratified in a non-trivial way.

Sex differences impact on occupational interests and achievement—differences that contribute greatly to the wage and social status advantage that men enjoy in most (if not all) industrialized nations. The acquisition of the educational credentials required for a lucrative career in a field such as engineering—a math-intensive field—is made easier for men by virtue of cognitive factors that are less pronounced for women.

And of course, as long as women carry, give birth, and nurture their offspring, they will be set at a social disadvantage and even face subjugation. As cyberfeminist Donna Haraway noted in her *Cyborg Manifesto*,

> ... control strategies applied to women's capacities to give birth to new human beings will be developed in the languages of population control and maximization of goal achievement for individual decision-makers. Control strategies will be formulated in terms of rates, costs of constraints, degrees of freedom. Human beings, like any other component or subsystem, must be localized in a system architecture whose basic modes of operation are probabilistic, statistical.

Consequently, Haraway saw true female liberation occurring through the application of cybernetics and the subsequent alleviation of biological pressures on women. As Haraway famously noted, "I'd rather be a cyborg than a goddess."

End of Immutable Sex Characteristics

While reproductively necessary, the ongoing presence of gender has proven problematic over time. Humanity is far removed from its evolutionary heritage and environment. More-

The Merger of Man and Machine

Experts are already getting ready for what they say could be a radical transformation of the human race in as little as two decades.

"This will happen faster than people realize," said Dr. Ray Kurzweil, an inventor and futurist who calculates technology trends using what he calls the law of accelerating returns, a mathematical concept that measures the exponential growth of technological evolution. . . .

Now, Kurzweil is predicting the arrival of something called the Singularity, which he defines as "the culmination of the merger of our biological thinking and existence with our technology, resulting in a world that is still human but that transcends our biological roots."

There will be no distinction, post-Singularity, between human and machine or between physical and virtual reality.

Lara Farrar, CNN.com,
July 15, 2008. www.cnn.com.

over, evolution makes for a poor moral compass. We value fairness, non-arbitrariness and egalitarianism—even in the genetic sphere; the ongoing presence of gender should therefore trouble us. We should strive for a post-Darwinian condition.

We are, often at a subconscious level, working to become postbiological. Most of us are in denial about or in opposition to this, but the level of control that we seek over our minds and bodies is in tune with this goal. We are perpetually working to transcend our biological vulnerabilities and constraints. This will eventually get us to the oft spoken and quasi-mythological posthuman condition.

Most efforts to achieve a postgendered state have largely focused on non-biological solutions, namely through social, educational, political and economic reform. While environmental strategies can be effective and important in their own right, they will continue to experience limited results on account of their inability to address the root of the problem: human biology.

Transhumanist postgenderism, as differentiated and further elucidated from mainstream feminism and postmodern/deconstructionist cyberfeminism, calls for *a more equitable distribution of gendered traits across the two sexes* and the *elimination of those gendered characteristics that are deemed disadvantageous.* Postgenderism in this form calls for actual reproductive and medical interventions for the achievement of these ends.

People deserve access to biotechnologies that will help them control their morphological, cognitive and reproductive characteristics. In a postgendered world, individuals will have the option to remain gendered, to experiment with their sex and sexuality, to mix and match gendered characteristics, or to reject gender altogether. *The idea is to exact control over our bodies and minds.* A postgendered condition does not necessarily imply the end of all gendered characteristics; it merely signifies the end of fixed and traditional gender assignments wrought by evolutionary processes. In this sense, persons who have undergone sexual reassignment surgery are humanity's first postgenderists.

There are other postgender biotechnologies in existence today. Birth control pills are a well established method that thwarts our reproductive natures, and menstruation suppression has all but arrived. Other physiological factors, such as hormonal influences and neurotransmitters, will soon be addressable.

Freedom from Gender Constraints

Looking ahead to the future, there's the possibility for male pregnancy and neurological interventions to normalize male and female cognitive functioning. More radical solutions to help persons become truly postgendered include the advent of artificial wombs, virtual reality and whole brain emulation.

At the social level, the broader suppressive and controlling social megastructure that exists and thrives on gender differences will be undermined by the postgenderist agenda. It will mark the end of sexual politics.

Thus, it is through the application of substantive and real biological interventions that the problem that is gender will most meaningfully be addressed. Postgender-tech will be an integral component to the larger collaborative struggle to achieve a genetically egalitarian, posthuman, and postbiological condition that works to the betterment of both individuals and society in general.

Periodical Bibliography

The following articles have been selected to supplement the diverse views presented in this chapter.

Jamaine Abidogun   "Western Education's Impact on Northern Igbo Gender Roles in Nsukka, Nigeria," *Africa Today*, Fall 2007.

Tania Branigan   "Straw: Future Laws to Be Gender Neutral," *Guardian (Manchester, UK)*, March 9, 2007.

Nancy Cruickshank   "Opinion: Social Media Can Reverse the Gender Imbalance in the Digital Sector," *Revolution*, December 4, 2008.

Nancy Gibbs   "Midlife Crisis? Bring It On!" *Time*, May 16, 2005.

Tamar Lewin   "At Colleges, Women Are Leaving Men in the Dust," *New York Times*, July 9, 2006.

Michael Shannon and Michael P. Kidd   "Projecting the U.S. Gender Wage Gap, 2000–2040," *Atlantic Economic Journal*, December 2003.

Rodrigo R. Soares and Bruno S.L. Falcao   "The Demographic Transition and the Sexual Division of Labor," *Journal of Political Economy*, December 2008.

Kristen Steagall   "Seeking a Post-gender Society," *University of Michigan Daily*, February 17, 2009.

John Tierney   "As Barriers Disappear, Some Gender Gaps Widen," *New York Times*, September 8, 2008.

Times of Zambia   "Zambia: Educators Must Teach Gender Issues," March 9, 2009.

Emma de Vita and Miranda Kennett   "Where Have All the IT Girls Gone?" *Management Today*, February 1, 2008.

For Further Discussion

Chapter 1

1. The nature-versus-nurture debate has been going on for ages and is not likely to be settled anytime soon. Does it have to be? What value would it be to society, if any, to discover that the differences in men and women's preferences and behavior are influenced by genes or upbringing? What value would it be to individuals, if any, to learn these things? Cite from the viewpoints in this chapter in your answers.

2. The viewpoints by Rosalind Barnett and Caryl Rivers and Lori Baker-Sperry both describe opposite-sex interactions among schoolchildren in school settings. Does one viewpoint present a more authentic representation than the other of how children behave? To what degree can an adult observer impartially describe children's gender behavior? Do the classroom reactions observed by Baker-Sperry support or undermine the arguments about boys and girls made by authors Barnett and Rivers? Explain.

3. Phil Dimitriadis argues that women can perform as well as men at Australian football, a team sport, while Amby Burfoot argues that women will never perform as well as men at running, an individual sport (although some women will always beat some men). How well do you think all-women teams could compete against all-men teams in the same sport? Can teams of skilled individuals make up for the differences in the average size and strength of men and women? Explain your answer, citing from the viewpoints.

Chapter 2

1. Currently, men produce the most technology even though women monopolize the use of some sectors of it, such as online shopping. Beyond the generic benefits to individual women who could find high-paying jobs in technology, is there any particular benefit to the technological industry for recruiting more women? Does it necessarily improve a service used mostly by women to have women making it? What benefits might arise (for individuals, society, or corporations) from having men design a product or service used mostly by women? Cite from the viewpoints presented in this chapter in answering these questions.

2. Much is made of the failure of the United States to have a female head of state when so many other countries have been run by women, even though some of those other countries do not have as large a population or the same election processes for heads of states. Is what other countries do relevant to America? To what extent is the failure of political parties to advance women candidates responsible for this situation? To what extent are U.S. voters? Consider especially the viewpoints by Matthew J. Streb et al. and Elayne Boosler when answering these questions.

Chapter 3

1. Marty Nemko suggests that fewer women than men are corporate leaders because fewer women are willing to make the same personal sacrifices to advance their careers. Joanna L. Krotz, however, suggests that women's particular talents are better suited than those of men for the kind of corporate culture the future requires. Is it fair to expect leaders to make significant personal sacrifices to advance an organization? If women are the needed leaders of the next generation of commerce, should corporate culture reexamine its own expectations and requirements for which people get promoted? How so or why not?

Chapter 4

1. In Western nations, and in many other rapidly moderniz-ing ones, men and women's fashions and behaviors are starting to greatly resemble each other. Does this mean that the boundaries between men and women are blur-ring? How much of a person's identity can be defined by clothing or habits? Are there essential physiological differ-ences between men and women that will never be over-come? Refer to the viewpoints by Chris Nutter and Boyé Lafayette De Mente, in particular, when answering these questions.

2. Marilyn Gardner and Alexandra Montgomery essentially make opposing arguments concerning the likelihood of gender equality in the future. In your view, does biology or socialization play the biggest part in gender inequality? One hundred and fifty years ago, no country allowed women to vote, yet almost every single nation today ac-knowledges that right. How long do you think the trend of improving women's political and social status will con-tinue? Do you think women will ever surpass men in in-fluence and power and reinstate gender inequality against men? Explain your answers.

Organizations to Contact

The editors have compiled the following list of organizations concerned with the issues debated in this book. The descriptions are derived from materials provided by the organizations. All have publications or information available for interested readers. The list was compiled on the date of publication of the present volume; the information provided here may change. Be aware that many organizations take several weeks or longer to respond to inquiries, so allow as much time as possible.

Families and Work Institute
267 Fifth Ave., Fl. 2, New York, NY   10016
(212) 465-2044 • fax: (212) 465-8637
e-mail: publications@familiesandwork.org
Web site: www.familiesandwork.org

The Families and Work Institute is a nonprofit organization that addresses the changing nature of work and family life. It is committed to finding research-based strategies to foster mutually supportive connections among workplaces, families, and communities. Research reports and other materials are available from the institute.

Family Research Council (FRC)
801 G Street NW, Washington, DC   20001
(202) 393-2100 • fax: (202) 393-2134
Web site: www.frc.org

FRC is an organization dedicated to the promotion of marriage and family and the sanctity of human life in national policy. Through books, pamphlets, media appearances, public events, debates, and testimony, the FRC reviews data and analyzes proposals that impact family law and policy in Congress and the executive branch. The FRC also strives to ensure the unique attributes of the family are recognized and respected through the decisions of the courts and regulatory bodies.

Fathers & Families
20 Park Plaza, Suite 628, Boston, MA   02116
(617) 542-9300 • fax: (617) 357-4911
e-mail: adminfaf@fathersandfamilies.org
Web site: www.fathersandfamilies.org

The mission of Fathers & Families is to improve the lives of children and strengthen society by protecting the child's right to the love and care of both parents after separation or divorce. The organization seeks better lives for children through family court reform that establishes equal rights and responsibilities for fathers and mothers. It works toward these goals with public relations and education campaigns, political lobbying, advocacy efforts, and research projects. The organization's Web site hosts a resource library on a variety of topics relating to parenting, custody, health, and statistics, and more general men's issues.

Fawcett Society
1–3 Berry Street, London, UK   EC1V 0AA
Web site: www.fawcettsociety.org.uk

Named for Millicent Fawcett, a leading proponent of women's suffrage in England in the 1860s, today's Fawcett Society works for the elimination of inequality between women and men. The society campaigns on women's representation in politics and public life; pay, pensions and poverty; valuing caring work; and the treatment of women in the justice system in the United Kingdom. To achieve these goals, the society runs public awareness campaigns, participates in political events and festivals, comments on government and public issues, and publishes the twice-yearly magazine *StopGap* and a free electronic newsletter.

The Howard Center
934 N. Main Street, Rockford, IL   61103
(815) 964-5819 • fax: (815) 965-1826
e-mail: info@profam.org
Web site: www.profam.org

The Howard Center works to return the United States to Judeo-Christian values and supports traditional families and gender roles. It studies the evolution of the family and the effects of divorce on society. The center offers a newsletter, blog, and several publications.

The Human Behavior and Evolution Society (HBES)
Web site: www.hbes.com

The Human Behavior and Evolution Society (HBES) is an interdisciplinary, international society of researchers, primarily from the social and biological sciences, who use modern evolutionary theory to help to discover human nature—including evolved emotional, cognitive, and sexual adaptations. The HBES hosts an annual conference that highlights new research and publishes the print journal *Evolution and Human Behavior* and the free online journal *Evolutionary Psychology: An International Journal of Evolutionary Approaches to Psychology and Behavior*, both of which are peer-reviewed.

Humanity+
PO Box 128, Willington, CT   06279
e-mail: secretary@transhumanism.org
Web site: http://humanityplus.org

Humanity+, formerly known as the World Transhumanist Association, is an international nonprofit membership organization that advocates the ethical use of technology to expand human capacities. It supports the development of and access to new technologies that enable everyone to enjoy better minds, better bodies, and better lives; members participate in two dozen chapters around the world. The organization's first accomplishment was writing the *Transhumanist Declaration* in 1998. It publishes *H+*, a quarterly magazine that covers the scientific, technological, and cultural changes that are transforming the human experience.

The International Society for Human Ethology (ISHE)
Web site: www.ishe.org

The ISHE aims at promoting ethological perspectives in the scientific study of humans worldwide. The core topics of ethology are fundamental and universal human behaviors such as infant attachment, emotion, dominance and other social relationships, nonverbal communication, courtship, and ritual. The ISHE publishes the quarterly *Human Ethology Bulletin*, which features book reviews, bibliographies, and discussion from its members. Every year the society holds a five-day congress. Its members are composed of researchers and students from a variety of academic disciplines ranging from anthropology and primatology to psychology and nursing.

The Lesbian, Gay, Bisexual & Transgender Community Center
208 W. Thirteenth Street, New York, NY   10011
(212) 620-7310 • fax: (212) 924-2657
Web site: www.gaycenter.org

The Lesbian, Gay, Bisexual & Transgender Community Center provides social and organization support and meeting space to individuals and groups in the lesbian, gay, bisexual, and transgender (LGBT) community. It provides everything from education and outreach to recreational programs and has political and advocacy arms that address issues and fight for the elimination of discrimination against LGBT people. Its Youth Enrichment Services and Gender Identity Project support people in the process of discovering and defining themselves and help them build communities. The center houses the historical archives of its LGBT community and makes them accessible for exhibits, publications, and scholarly research activities.

National Coalition for Men (NCFM)
932 C Street, Suite B, San Diego, CA   92101
(888) 223-1280
e-mail: ncfm@ncfm.org
Web site: www.ncfm.org

The NCFM promotes awareness of how gender-based expectations limit men legally, socially, and psychologically. The organization suggests that just as sex-stereotyping has limited the potential of women, it has also confined men to expected roles regardless of their individual abilities, interests, physical/ emotional constitutions, or needs. The NCFM promotes the discussion and study of relevant issues, disseminates information, facilitates the development of new resources, and sponsors topical meetings, workshops, and lectures.

National Organization for Women (NOW)
1100 H Street NW, 3rd Fl., Washington, DC   20005
(202) 628-8669 • fax: (202) 785-8576
Web site: www.now.org

NOW is the largest, most comprehensive feminist advocacy group in the United States. Its purpose is to take action to bring women into full participation in society—sharing equal rights, responsibilities, and opportunities with men, while living free from discrimination. NOW organizes rallies, protests, demonstrations, and marches; lobbies for and writes laws that promote the full equality of women; forms alliances with other organizations; and hosts a national conference. There are NOW chapters in all fifty states.

Bibliography of Books

Michelle Ann
Abate

Tomboys: A Literary and Cultural History. Philadelphia: Temple University Press, 2008.

Rebecca Kay
Basingstoke, ed.

Gender, Equality and Difference During and After State Socialism. New York: Palgrave, 2007.

Thomas Beatie

Labor of Love: The Story of One Man's Extraordinary Pregnancy. Berkeley, CA: Seal Press, 2008.

Harry M.
Benshoff and
Sean Griffin

America on Film: Representing Race, Class, Gender, and Sexuality at the Movies. 2nd ed. Hoboken, NJ: Wiley-Blackwell, 2009.

Francine D. Blau,
Mary C. Brinton,
and David B.
Grusky, eds.

Declining Significance of Gender. New York: Russell Sage Foundation, 2006.

Shmuley Boteach

The Broken American Male: And How to Fix Him. New York: St. Martin's Press, 2008.

Anne K. Boulis
and Jerry A.
Jacobs

The Changing Face of Medicine: Women Doctors and the Evolution of Health Care in America. Ithaca, NY: Cornell University Press, 2008.

Anne R.
Breneman and
Ruth A. Mbuh,
eds.

Women in the New Millennium: The Global Revolution. Lanham, MD: Hamilton Books, 2006.

Stephanie A. Brill and Rachel Pepper — *The Transgender Child: A Handbook for Families and Professionals.* San Francisco: Cleis Press, 2008.

Jude Browne, ed. — *The Future of Gender.* New York: Cambridge University Press, 2007.

Terri Casey — *Pride and Joy: The Lives and Passions of Women Without Children.* New York: Simon & Schuster, 2007.

Sarah Chase — *Perfectly Prep: Gender Extremes at a New England Prep School.* New York: Oxford University Press, 2008.

Neil Chethik — *VoiceMale: What Husbands Really Think About Their Marriages, Their Wives, Sex, Housework, and Commitment.* New York: Simon & Schuster, 2008.

David Coad — *The Metrosexual: Gender, Sexuality, and Sport.* Albany: State University of New York Press, 2008.

Jocelyn Elise Crowley — *Defiant Dads: Fathers' Rights Activists in America.* Ithaca, NY: Cornell University Press, 2008.

Susan Dewey — *Making Miss India Miss World: Constructing Gender, Power, and the Nation in Postliberalization India.* Syracuse, NY: Syracuse University Press, 2008.

Jeanne Flavin — *Our Bodies, Our Crimes: The Policing of Women's Reproduction in America.* New York: New York University Press, 2009.

Richard K. Francis — *Why Men Won't Ask for Directions: The Seductions of Sociobiology.* Princeton, NJ: Princeton University Press, 2004.

Guy Garcia — *The Decline of Men: How the American Male Is Tuning Out, Giving Up, and Flipping Off His Future.* New York: HarperCollins, 2009.

David Gauntlett — *Media, Gender and Identity: An Introduction.* New York: Routledge, 2008.

Anne Marie Goetz, ed. — *Governing Women: Women's Political Effectiveness in Contexts of Democratization and Governance Reform.* New York: Routledge, 2009.

Elyse Goldstein — *The New Jewish Feminism: Probing the Past, Forging the Future.* Woodstock, VT: Jewish Lights, 2008.

Geoffry Greif — *Buddy System: Understanding Male Friendships.* New York: Oxford University Press, 2008.

Michael Gurian and Barbara Annis — *Leadership and the Sexes: Using Gender Science to Create Success in Business.* San Francisco: Jossey-Bass, 2008.

Joan Huber — *On the Origins of Gender Inequality.* Boulder, CO: Paradigm, 2007.

Michael S. Kimmel and Michael A. Messner, eds. — *Men's Lives.* 7th ed. Boston: Pearson, Allyn and Bacon, 2007.

Kathleen Parker   *Save the Males: Why Men Matter, Why Women Should Care.* New York: Random House, 2008.

Angelo Pezzote   *Straight Acting: Gay Men, Masculinity, and Finding True Love.* New York: Kensington, 2008.

Susan Pinker   *The Sexual Paradox: Extreme Men, Gifted Women and the Real Gender Gap.* Mississauga, ON: Random House Canada, 2008.

Lionel Tiger   *Men in Groups.* New Brunswick, NJ: Transaction, 2005.

Trent Watts, ed.   *White Masculinity in the Recent South.* Baton Rouge: Louisiana State University Press, 2008.

Index